Teaching Physical Education

a Guide for Mentors and Students

Anne Williams

David Fulton Publishers
London

David Fulton Publishers Ltd
2 Barbon Close, London WC1N 3JX

First published in Great Britain by David Fulton Publishers 1996

British Library Cataloguing in Publication Data

A catalogue record for this book is available from the British Library

ISBN 1-85346-427-9

Typeset by Textype Typesetters, Cambridge
Printed in Great Britain by BPC Books and Journals Ltd, Exeter

Contents

Series Editor's Foreword v

1 Introduction 1

2 The Teaching Process 17

3 Planning for Effective Teaching 24

4 Teaching Styles 43

5 Teaching Strategies 56

6 Assessing Pupils 66

7 Entitlement to Learning for All – Equal Opportunity Issues ... 79

8 Helping Students to Learn from Observation 89

9 Collaborative Teaching 98

10 Observing Lessons and Giving Feedback 104

11 Assessing Teaching Competence 119

Further Reading/References 125

Index 129

QUALITY IN SECONDARY SCHOOLS AND COLLEGES SERIES

Series Editor: Clyde Chitty

This series publishes on a wide range of topics related to successful education for the 11–19 age group. It reflects the growing interest in whole-school curriculum planning together with the effective teaching of individual subjects and themes. There are also books devoted to management and administration, examinations and assessment, pastoral care strategies, relationships with parents and governors and the implications for schools of changes in teacher education. Titles include:

Active History in Key Stages 3 and 4
Alan Farmer and Peter Knight
1-85346-305-1

The Emerging 16-19 Curriculum: Policy and Provision
Jeremy Higham, Paul Sharp and David Yeomans
1-85346-389-2

English and Ability
Edited by Andrew Goodwyn
1-85346-299-3

English and the OFSTED Experience
Bob Bibby and Barrie Wade (with Trevor Dickinson)
1-85346-357-4

Geography 11-16: Rekindling Good Practice
Bill Marsden
1-85346-296-9

Heeding Heads: Secondary Heads and Educational Commentators in Dialogue
Edited by David Hustler, Tim Brighouse and Jean Rudduck
1-85346-358-2

Learning to Teach: a Guide for School-based Initial and In-Service Training
Julian Stern
1-85346-371-X

The Literate Imagination: Renewing the Secondary English Curriculum
Bernard T. Harrison
1-85346-300-0

Managing the Learning of History
Richard Brown
1-85346-345-0

Moral Education through English 11-16
Ros McCulloch and Margaret Mathieson
1-85346-276-4

The New Teacher: An Introduction to Teaching in Comprehensive Education
Nigel Tubbs
1-85346-424-4

Partnership in Secondary Initial Teacher Education
Edited by Anne Williams
1-85346-361-2

School Improvement: What Can Pupils Tell Us?
Edited by Jean Rudduck, Roland Chaplain and Gwen Wallace
1-85346-393-0

Valuing English: Reflections on the National Curiculum
Roger Knight
1-85346-374-4

Series Editor's Foreword

This book offers guidance and support for those physical education teachers who are asked to become involved with the initial training of PE student teachers. It is written at a time when student teachers spend longer in the schools and schools are assuming a more generous responsibility for some of the training activities previously undertaken by colleges and universities. It is clear that the mentor's role is both complex and challenging, and this book provides many helpful suggestions for approaching the role in a constructive and positive fashion. Much satisfaction can be derived from seeing student teachers develop in confidence, as well as from being required to re-think theory and practice on a regular basis.

Clyde Chitty
May 1996

CHAPTER 1

Introduction

This book is written to provide a resource for those involved with the support and training of PE student teachers. Although students will be the responsibility of a designated member of a department who is their mentor, the most successful placements tend to be those where all members of the department play an active role in the support of the student. The book will also provide reference material for students and for tutors who are working with mentors in the developing partnerships. The focus is upon ways of supporting student learning both by outlining the issues involved in the development of different aspects of teaching competence and by suggesting practical strategies for working with students in order to help their development as teachers to progress. It is written in the belief that different students learn in different ways and respond differently to specific approaches. Some need a great deal of reassurance that they are 'doing OK'. Others want to know everything that needs to be 'put right' at the end of their first attempt at teaching. Some want to spend all their time in front of classes. Others want opportunities to observe, followed by a supported introduction to small group teaching before they feel ready to face a class. Some of these differences reflect different personalities, levels of confidence and so on. Some reflect the student's previous experience.

While physical education staff have always played an important role in supporting student teachers, the changed context within which teachers are now working with students means that the role has both changed and extended. It has extended because of requirements that students spend longer in schools and changed because schools have now assumed a greater responsibility for some of the training activities formerly undertaken by universities and colleges. Some schools have chosen to take total responsibility for student training. This book offers guidance for physical education teachers who are asked to work with students in this brave new world of initial teacher education.

Being a mentor

Why be a mentor?

Many teachers enjoy working with student teachers and derive considerable satisfaction from seeing their development as prospective teachers. There is thus considerable job satisfaction to be gained. Being a mentor can also contribute to the professional development of the teacher. This can happen in a variety of ways. Teachers often refer to the fact that contact with students and with higher education brings them into contact with new ideas and resources. Being observed by someone else can have a motivating effect on one's own practice. Perhaps most important, the process of analysing and articulating one's own practice in a form which is accessible to a questioning student, has a very positive effect on understanding of one's own teaching.

What is involved?

Many though not all mentors are heads of departments. Being mentor and head of department has the advantage of status which can help in negotiation with senior school staff as well as in the development of a whole department approach to work with students and in the influencing of other colleagues. The disadvantage is that heads of department are invariably already very busy. Other members of a department can be very effective mentors, but will need the head of department's support. They should be good role models, that is, their own experience and expertise should be such that students can learn about a range of teaching approaches, about good class management and about teaching the National Curriculum across a range of activity areas.

Mentors need knowledge, skills and attributes. A successful teacher is not automatically a successful trainer of students which is essentially about working with adult learners rather than with children. Adult learners including student teachers generally bring considerable expertise, experience, as well as knowledge and skills, in contrast with children who may not bring such attributes. However the student teacher is new to learning about teaching and is likely to embark on a course with certain preconceptions or assumptions about teaching and what they need to do in order to become a teacher.

Most students will be heavily influenced by their past experience both as pupils and as students. This can lead to very narrow views of teaching and learning which may militate against their ability to adapt to changing circumstances. While students will learn a great deal through practice, their learning will be influenced by the quality of the help they get, the sorts of practice involved and the supplementing of that practice with other activities such as structured observations and seminars, workshops and discussions.

Below are some of the things which mentors could or should do. The extent to which some of them come within the mentor's remit will depend upon how particular partnerships have agreed to share the responsibility for the students' learning. Others would apply to all training models.

Planning

Students need to feel

- welcome
- supported and confident
- successful
- that they are continuing to learn.

This involves

- planning prior to their arrival
- planning for successful early visits/days – first impressions count
- planning programmes which meet their needs and course requirements, which build on earlier placements (where relevant), which offer manageable challenges and which include the right balance of observing, teaching, preparation time, thinking time and meeting/discussion time
- planning for ongoing monitoring and support based upon constructive observation and feedback
- planning specific training activities which will support their further learning
- support by mentors who want to do it and who are well prepared and equipped for their task.

Guidance and support

The kinds of **guidance** needed will depend upon the stage of the student's training and on their experience and expertise. It could well involve guidance about planning:

> We sat down once a week and went through my plans. It meant that I could be confident that, with a bit of luck, provided I got it right on the day, at least the content and organisation should be OK. I found it really helpful.

Planning is discussed further in Chapter 3. Lesson planning has, in the past, often been the responsibility of the university, but, in most courses today, it will either be a shared commitment or one which falls largely upon the school.

Provision of **advice** is also important and this can come from different people, provided that the student is able to cope with assessing the advice given and deciding which has to be acted upon and where there is scope for choice. The student will obviously seek advice from the mentor but also needs access to advice from others. This may be other teachers within the school or it may be through meeting up with other students either as part of consortium arrangements or during their return to their higher education institution.

Listening is an important way of providing support.

> My Head of Department was always prepared to listen to me even when she had different ideas from mine.

Listening involves both adopting an approach which sees the student as having views, thoughts, problems and so on which he or she needs to talk about and then finding time to actually do it.

Brooks et al. (1994) make the point that it is all too easy for student teachers to fall into a 'dependency' mode which can unwittingly be encouraged by mentors who are used to institutions where the pupil–adult relationship fosters a dependency culture even where independent and responsible behaviour is expected of pupils.

> The tendency to talk at passive students is overwhelming at times. I learnt more when I listened.

Feedback from students on their school placements indicates very clearly that the need to feel **supported** by their mentor is very important. Adult learners may well feel very vulnerable on being placed in a learning situation which carries what may appear to be daunting expectations. Few are willing to admit to feelings of vulnerability. Mentors and other teachers working with students need to remind themselves of the possibility of such feelings even when there is no overt evidence of their existence. For some students, learning to teach may well be the first time that they have attempted to do something where success can be elusive. Learning to teach can be a very isolated process.

> I felt that I should not have been placed on my own. Support is essential during school placements.

Many partnerships are now placing students in pairs which means that they may be able to support and motivate each other but this depends upon their compatibility.

Support can also take the form of **encouraging** the student to become **independent** within the limits of departmental and school policies. It is important that students are encouraged to develop their own style of teaching and that those observing assess what goes on in terms of whether it works and not whether it is how the observer would have done it. Brooks et al. (1994) describe mentors who saw students as contributing to everyone's professional development through a two way exchange of ideas which would foster the student's professional independence.

> They've participated in departmental meetings which are a fairly open forum for discussion of ideas. They've joined in that very effectively. Ideas that they've produced in their teaching which have been particularly effective, we do tend to discuss and utilise. They've added those to the general pool.

The effective mentor will appreciate that there is no one correct way to teach and that what works for one person and in one school may not be the answer in a different context or for a different teacher. Part of **encouraging review and reflection** is therefore to help the student to put his or her performance in context.

> He always asked me to think about whether that activity had worked by luck or good planning and whether it would work with other groups that I taught or had seen.

Promoting student learning and progress

Students need **opportunities to observe practice**, but it is important that these opportunities are structured carefully to meet student needs and that they have a clearly defined and explicit focus. Chapter 8 looks at how to make good use of observation.

Most partnerships have expectations in terms of the number of lessons which the mentor should **observe** and on which he or she should **provide feedback**. Written feedback is expected on a given number of lessons during a placement. This is usually much appreciated by students who find that oral feedback, although useful, is too often forgotten. Written feedback not only provides valuable help with future planning and teaching but it also contributes to recording student progress.

> I had detailed and constructive criticism which really helped me to improve.

Approaches to feedback on lessons are considered in Chapter 10.

Team or collaborative teaching is a potentially powerful learning tool which is discussed in Chapter 9. Now that students are in school for longer periods of time, there is plenty of opportunity for whole class solo teaching and it is easier to build in team teaching activities. These may involve teaching with an experienced teacher or it may involve a pair of students sharing responsibility for a class.

> I would have liked more opportunity for team teaching where I could have learnt from working with someone more experienced.

Monitoring, reviewing and recording progress

Discussion of their current progress and **setting targets** is important, particularly to ensure that students achieve their potential rather than just achieving a very basic level of competence. Regular meetings with students, which should be built into all student programmes enable targets to be reviewed regularly. Target setting is discussed in Chapter 10.

Although schools have always been expected to report on the students placed with them, the transfer of most of the responsibility for the **formal assessment** of the student has caused anxieties in many schools. The potential conflict between the role of supporter and helper and that of assessor has concerned many mentors. Assessment of students is discussed in Chapter 11.

Some mentors may be invited to participate in the **selection** of students for initial teacher education courses. Some may be asked to join groups or committees to contribute to **course planning, development** or **audit**.

What does the mentor need to know before the students arrive?

- *Information about the course which the students are following*. Unless trained very recently, there are likely to be very significant differences in mentors' training and that of the students.
- *Expectations of the mentor and of the rest of the department?* Different partnerships have different expectations of students and, consequently, of mentors, and students may be placed at different stages of their training and from different courses. Clearly what is expected of a first year student on a four year course will be very different from that expected from a final year student or from a PGCE student on a second placement. Does everyone in the department know what is expected of them? Are they expected to complete observation sheets on students' teaching? What will their role be in the assessment of the student? Will everyone in the department be involved? Equally?
- *How much is known about the students who are to be placed?* Many institutions have mechanisms whereby students contact the school in advance of their first visit or the school is supplied with information about the student. If this does not happen, or if the information is incomplete, maybe this can be raised at a mentors' meeting.
- *Is the information which students will need available?* Students will generally have a checklist of information which they need to collect in order to go away and do their own preparation and planning. Some information is directly related to the teaching which the student will be doing, while some may be needed in order that the student can complete assignments required by the HEI. The sorts of things which may be needed include:

- Departmental syllabuses/schemes of work
- Departmental procedures
  - access to activity areas
  - showers
  - jewellery
  - accidents
  - non-participants
- Departmental policies
  - equal opportunities
  - assessment
  - extra-curricular activities
  - resources and their availability
  - rewards and sanctions
- Reprographics
- IT
- Equipment and facilities

Being a student

Training to be a teacher is different from training for almost any other profession in that all students already have considerable experience of schools – as pupils. It may be worth spending a few minutes reflecting upon this experience and considering what might be learnt from it.

> I remember loads of kids hated PE at our school – it was OK for me 'cos I was really good at it and got plenty of help and attention but he was really sarky with these poor lads who missed the ball or never got into a position to get it in the first place. No wonder they wagged school on PE days! I've always thought that if I become a teacher I'll want to be there for all the kids, not just the three or four good ones.

> What I'll always remember is that I got dropped from the netball team one week because I hadn't been to either of the practices. I was the shooter and I knew that I was much better than anyone else so I didn't need to practise. It really served me right for being such a bighead and I'll never forget my teacher saying to me 'There are plenty of people who'd be glad of half your ability, but I want people playing who'll give 110%, not someone who thinks she's doing us a favour.

> I loved every minute of it and I can't think of anything better than helping a whole lot of kids to get the same kind of enjoyment and achievement.

Becoming a teacher

What is expected of a newly qualified teacher?

The Department for Education describes the competences expected of newly qualified teachers under five headings given below. The application of the competences within physical education is outlined briefly.

'Newly qualified teachers should be able to demonstrate:

- an understanding of the knowledge, concepts and skills of their specialist subjects and of the place of these subjects in the school curriculum;

What knowledge of the National Curriculum activity area does the student bring to their course? The school leaver embarking upon a four year course may have followed a broad curriculum through their school career or a very narrow one. The postgraduate student may have followed an undergraduate course which includes a generous practical component or one which is minimal. Furthermore the practical programme followed may be in activities which are relevant to the school curriculum but they need not be. The opportunities which the postgraduate has taken, to follow courses on their own initiative may well contribute more to their knowledge of physical education activity areas than did their undergraduate courses.

Is the student aware of the place of physical education as a National Curriculum subject in the school curriculum? This implies awareness of the core and foundation subjects and of the requirements for their study at the various Key Stages. In order to understand this, the student needs to be familiar with the terminology of the National Curriculum, for example, Attainment Targets, Programmes of Study, Key Stages (and their associated years), End of Key Stage Descriptors.

Is the student aware of cross-curricular themes and dimensions and of the contribution which physical education can or should make to these? Health education is the most obvious example of a cross-curricular theme to which physical education should make a significant contribution although it is not the only one. For example, outdoor and adventurous activities offer many opportunities to address environmental education.

- knowledge and understanding of the National Curriculum and attainment targets (NCATs) and the programmes of study (PoS) in the subjects they are preparing to teach, together with an understanding of the framework of the statutory requirements;

Is the student aware of the National Curriculum requirements of physical education at the Key Stages for which he or she is preparing? Can the student interpret End of Key Stage Descriptors in the context of particular activity Programmes of Study?

- breadth and depth of subject knowledge extending beyond PoS and examination syllabuses in school;

What knowledge of the National Curriculum activity areas does the student bring to their course? How will the student improve their knowledge of games, gymnastics, dance, athletics, swimming, outdoor and adventurous activities? How can the school and the mentor help with this?

Does the student have an adequate knowledge base in the academic study of physical education, that is, in those areas which constitute significant parts of GCSE, A level or GNVQ?

In what ways does the student's knowledge extend beyond Programmes of Study or examination syllabuses? In the context of physical education, this question may be answered in different ways. Unlike some other subject specialisms, there is not an expectation that all physical education teachers will be able to teach A level. Indeed the content of some relevant undergraduate courses is specialised with the result that some students will not have sufficient knowledge to be able to teach all aspects of A level. This is nevertheless a perfectly legitimate way in which a student could demonstrate knowledge at depth. An alternative could be through high level sport performance and understanding in one or in a range of activities.

Subject application

'Newly qualified teachers should be able to:

- produce coherent lesson plans which take account of NCATs and of the school's curriculum policies;

Students should be expected to produce lessons plans which take account of NCATs and of departmental schemes of work. They should demonstrate awareness of the relationship between a specific activity aim and NCATs. Chapter 3 gives more detailed guidance on planning.

It is easy for experienced teachers to forget just how much they take for granted in their own planning or to underestimate the amount of 'automatic' planning which comes with experience. Students can easily underestimate the amount of preparation which they will need to undertake, having seen it all look easy when observing a successful lesson taught by a confident, experienced and knowledgeable teacher.

- ensure continuity and progression within and between classes and in subjects;

Lesson plans over a period of time should address issues of continuity and progression. Appropriate expectations should be set for all pupils. This is a challenge for experienced teachers. Given the wide range of ability and developmental age present in many physical education lessons, differentiation is essential if challenging but manageable expectations are to be set for all. Teachers can help students' understanding by giving them the opportunity to observe classes in different years working on the same activity. It is important that there is discussion of what has been observed. Sometimes the same task may be set for two different age groups but with very different expectations in terms of outcome. The student, hearing the same task, may not appreciate what these expectations are, especially if his or her attention has focused on an able younger pupil and a less able older one.

– recognise the ways in which pupils develop and learn;

This involves an understanding of child development. In the context of physical education, there are many important issues about the physical development of young children which the student needs to know and apply in practice. For example, the physical changes which take place at puberty affect the kinds of activity which are appropriate. Knowledge of the age at which pupils are likely to reach puberty and of gender differences is important because of the implications for the range of ability within classes, especially mixed sex classes at Key Stage 3. An appreciation of the way bone growth takes place and of the implications for avoiding overuse injury among young people should inform decisions about physical tasks.

There is a considerable body of knowledge about the learning of physical skills which should inform the student's teaching. How physical skills are learned and the factors which affect this learning, including, for example, the effects of different sorts of feedback, of different patterns of practice, or the effects of success and failure are all-important. For example decisions about whether to offer pupils an intensive swimming course or a series of lessons spread over a period of time should be made in the context of what is known about distribution of practice. When deciding upon teaching styles to be used, understanding of the relationship between type of skill (e.g. closed or open) and learning approach (e.g. practice or problem-solving) will contribute to more effective learning.

In addition to the physiological and psychological dimensions mentioned above, there are many other factors which can affect pupil learning especially in the short term. Circumstances at home; incidents elsewhere in the school during an earlier lesson or at breaktime; relationships with peers can all affect behaviour and learning in specific lessons.

– set appropriately demanding expectations for pupils;

This implies both knowledge of what can reasonably be expected of pupils at different stages and an ability to use differentiation to ensure that all pupils are challenged. Approaches to differentiation are discussed in Chapter 3. Students' own background will almost certainly have been one of success in physical challenges even in activities where students perceive themselves to be weak. They therefore begin their course of training with little experience of the 'average' pupil. Their understanding of what should be expected of pupils is likely to be heavily influenced by the school experiences which they have during the course of their training. This places a considerable responsibility upon teachers who need to know how their pupils' attainment compares with those in other schools, both locally and nationally.

– employ a range of teaching strategies appropriate to the age ability and attainment levels of pupils;

In teaching lessons, students should be able to demonstrate a range of teaching strategies and styles, such as demonstration, explanation, questioning, guided practice, review and evaluation. Evidence could consist of the effective use of pupils to demonstrate a handstand. Other pupils are positioned so that they can see, are given specific points to look for and are questioned about these. The student could use questions to revise work on the use of the dig, the set and the volley in a game of volleyball. There should also be awareness of a range of teaching styles and an ability to use several, such as practice, reciprocal, problem-solving.

Consideration should also be given to the extent to which the student selects styles and strategies which are appropriate and safe. For example, problem-solving as an approach to a risk activity such as somersaulting skills in trampolining would be neither safe nor appropriate. The use of a pupil to demonstrate a pass in basketball, when there is no-one in the class capable of performing the skill in such a way that the required points can be emphasised, might be safe, but would not aid learning and would therefore be inappropriate.

– present subject knowledge in clear language and a stimulating manner;

The language used by the student should be relevant to the class being taught. Some students can find it difficult to adjust their vocabulary to the level of the pupils particularly when faced with children who have language difficulties.

– contribute to the development of pupils' language and communication skills;

This has implications for teaching styles in that in order to achieve the above, students need to adopt approaches which will give pupils opportunities both for listening and comprehension and for speaking and discussion. Teaching styles are discussed in Chapter 4.

– demonstrate the ability to select and use appropriate resources including Information Technology;

The effective selection and use of resources and equipment is part of the management skill of the teacher and it is perhaps artificial to separate resource use from management. Suffice to say that without the necessary organisational skills the student is unlikely to make effective use of resources. Many examples could be given of students who use a limited amount of equipment because they lack confidence in their ability to organise the use of more.

Use of IT remains embryonic in many PE departments. This is one area where students may well be able to help the teacher. Although many PE departments still have limited access to computers for their sole use, all can access the school's facilities. The use of IT to produce high quality written materials is within the capability of all, whether these be for notices for display or for worksheets to be used in the teaching situation. The development of multi media and increasing availability of multi media machines in schools will open up many new possibilities, particularly in the use of IT to support examination work.

Classroom management

'Newly qualified teachers should be able to:

- decide when teaching the whole class, groups, pairs or individuals is appropriate for particular learning purposes;

The effective use of a range of class organisational arrangements, i.e. whole class teaching, small group work, individual work or pair work should be assessed in relation to particular learning purposes. These may be introducing new skills, revising and developing skills, developing the ability to assess self and others, developing knowledge and understanding or developing personal and social skills. For the student, the ability to make sensible decisions is closely related to the development of observational skills, especially when deciding whether feedback is needed to the whole class, to groups or to individuals.

- create and maintain a purposeful and orderly environment for the pupils;

The creation of a purposeful and orderly environment in the context of physical education includes many aspects related to safety. Can the student use equipment safely? Is he or she aware of safety issues with respect to pupils, e.g. dress, jewellery, safe use of space, timing of activity so that fatigue does not become a safety issue and so on? Does the student have sufficient observational skills to maintain a safe learning environment? For example, does the student notice that netballs are about to blow onto the playing area: or that pupils have moved a piece of gymnastics equipment so that it is obstructing the landing area of an adjacent group? Is the student aware of the need for good organisation to ensure safety, e.g. pupils properly positioned for throwing events in athletics, groups given enough room to land and recover safely in the gymnasium? If there is an accident does the student know what to do?

- devise and use appropriate rewards and sanctions to maintain a safe learning environment;

Does the student use rewards and sanctions appropriately? Is physical activity used as a punishment in situations where this is inappropriate? For example, where pupils are not well motivated towards physical activity, punishments such as running round the playing field are unlikely to be conducive to encouraging a more positive attitude towards exercise.

– maintain pupils' interest and motivation;

Is the student aware of factors which affect pupils' behaviour such as external factors, motivation or class organisation? Can he or she use such knowledge to maintain interest and motivation?

What constitutes a behaviour problem? Is it specific to your school (e.g. pupils wearing patterned T-shirts when the rules state a white top), or generalisable to all schools (e.g. persistently interrupting when the teacher is talking)?

Is the student aware of a range of possible strategies to deal with problem behaviour, e.g.

- eye contact
- changing position to be physically close to pupil or pupils being disruptive
- deliberately ignoring the pupil
- removing temptation (the ball being played with) or moving the pupil (away from the apparatus)
- reinforcing class rules and routines (sit down, look this way and listen)
- sitting pupil out for a short time then inviting him or her back on condition that behaviour improves
- referral to class teacher or to more senior member of staff.

Is the student aware of when these different strategies would be appropriate?

Assessment recording and reporting

'Newly qualified teachers should be able to:

– identify the current level of attainment of individual pupils using NCATs, statements of attainment and end of key stage statements where applicable;

Since NCATs and EKSDs refer to performance at the end of a Key Stage, identification of Attainment Levels during the course of the Key Stage is not easy, especially in a subject where there are no levels for guidance. Students and teachers need to understand clearly what is involved in the learning of any given activity and what indicators would be useful in signalling level of performance at a particular stage. They also need to appreciate which NCATs or EKSDs are being addressed by that activity so that performance within it can be located in the wider context. Departmental schemes of work should indicate what is to be expected of pupils at the end of any given unit of work and these can help the student to compare individual pupil performance against these expectations.

- judge how well each pupil performs against the standard expected of a pupil of that age;

There are many who consider that this is an unreasonable expectation of a newly qualified teacher. Others believe that it is neither possible nor helpful to attempt such assessments given the range of variables which would affect different pupils in different contexts combined with developmental factors which will lead to pupils of the same age performing differently. Certainly in the physical education context, where there can be a physical developmental range of up to five years within a single class, such judgements are of limited value, particularly within a Key Stage which spans three school years.

- assess and record systematically the progress of individual pupils;

Are students aware of record-keeping systems used in their school and department? Many of these are based upon the class register which is used for recording, not only attendance, but the focus of individual lessons, whether the pupil participated, and how successfully. Contributing to this process can be the pupil's Record of Achievement which enables each individual to assess his or her performance together with other related elements such as effort, enjoyment, targets for the future and so on.

- use such assessment in their teaching;

An integral part of the teaching process is the feedback which teachers give to pupils through the course of all lessons. Assessments made of pupils should guide planning of subsequent lessons, particularly in making decisions about the suitability of tasks for the whole class and about extension work for the able or simplified tasks for those who are struggling (see Chapter 4 on differentiation).

- demonstrate that they understand the importance of reporting to pupils on their progress and of marking their work regularly against agreed criteria;

Reporting progress to pupils is really covered by earlier statements in that records of progress should be made known to pupils and feedback to them on their progress should be an integral part of every lesson. Reporting to parents occurs generally through parents evenings, end of term reports and Records of Achievement. Students should be familiar with the school's policy. This may be the subject mentor's task or it may be covered as part of a wider issues programme within the school.

Further professional development

Newly qualified teachers should have acquired in initial training the necessary foundation to develop:

- an understanding of the school as an institution and its place within the community;
- a working knowledge of their pastoral, contractual, legal and administrative responsibilities;
- an ability to develop effective working relationships with professional colleagues and parents and to develop their communication skills;
- an awareness of individual differences, including the social, psychological, developmental and cultural dimensions;
- the ability to recognise diversity of talent including that of gifted pupils;
- the ability to identify special educational needs or learning difficulties;
- a self-critical approach to diagnosing and evaluating pupils' learning, including a recognition of the effects of that learning on teachers' expectations;
- a readiness to promote the moral and spiritual well-being of pupils.'

Some of these headings have a more obvious subject specific dimension than others. For example, the identification of special educational needs needs to be examined in the physical education context because there are many pupils who have special educational needs in physical education which are unique to performance in that subject. Other pupils with special educational needs in the classroom may be able to work in the physical education context more independently and successfully. The issues of entitlement for all pupils including those with special educational needs is discussed in Chapter 7.

These competences have been criticised by some teachers as neglecting important personal qualities which all teachers need. The following attributes have been drawn from a number of texts on effective teaching:

humorous	enthusiastic	enjoys the subject
relaxed	organised	makes the work relevant
imaginative	supportive	is active in helping pupils learn
warm	cheerful	uses a variety of methods
firm	flexible	has high expectations
friendly	encourages	explains clearly
listens	sympathetic	gives praise
fair	responsive	applies sanctions fairly and doesn't make empty threats

(From Capel, Leask and Turner, 1995, p23)

It is therefore clear that the mentor's role is complex and challenging. He or she will be involved in various ways in helping students to acquire a wide range of competences and to capitalise on personal qualities which they bring to teaching. The successful mentor will almost certainly involve the whole department in the process and will enable the student to contribute to the department as well as learning from it. It is worth remembering that the mentor role is also a rewarding one both personally through the satisfaction of seeing new teachers develop in confidence as well as in competence and professionally through the ongoing development which comes from thinking about and articulating one's own practice and from having it challenged by enquiring minds.

CHAPTER 2

The Teaching Process

Students and NQTs' continued development as teachers depends, in the medium and long term, upon their ability to analyse their own practice and make changes in the light of this analysis. They and their mentors need an understanding of this process, currently described in much of the literature as reflective practice. This chapter will begin by considering what is meant by 'the reflective teacher'. It will then look at the teaching process in physical education.

What kind of teachers?

Much initial and in-service teacher education is based upon a philosophy of reflective practice. Exactly what this means is less clear. Since reflective practice has become a 'bandwagon' term in educational jargon, it is worth spending a few moments considering the different meanings of reflective practice. Mawer makes the point that teaching is seen as an art by some and a science by others and provides a useful overview of different thinking about this issue (Mawer, 1995). Clearly one's view of the nature of teaching will affect attitudes to and definitions of reflection.

At the most basic level, there would be general agreement that good teaching involves ongoing development of styles and techniques based upon judgements made about the effectiveness or otherwise of existing practice. It means asking whether what is currently being done is working. As new approaches are developed, new materials and resources appear and new initiatives are introduced there is always a need for decision-making. Do we get involved with GNVQ? with A level PE? Should we rethink our approaches to pupil groupings? Is this new gymnastics equipment going to be a good investment? That small group in Year 9 is becoming a real problem – what am I going to do to try and improve their motivation? All teachers are thus expected to be reflective in some ways. The introduction of appraisal formalises this in terms of the teacher's own performance by asking them to consider their achievements and difficulties in the context of ongoing staff development.

Taking this a stage further means asking more fundamental questions about your teaching and continuing to question throughout your teaching career. This means asking questions about what is worth doing. Should my priority be to encourage participation by everyone in extracurricular clubs or should I be concentrating on the school team? Am I really providing equal opportunity for boys and girls? Which National Curriculum activity areas are the most appropriate for this school?

Unreflective teaching means that you do things because they've always been done that way; because that is how college taught you to do it; because that's how they do it at the school down the road; because I've never really thought about the alternatives.

What then might reflective teaching mean for the student?

One interpretation is that reflection is a utilitarian tool involving putting into practice research findings and theoretical formulations of education. That is, the reflective process helps teachers to reproduce classroom practices found, by empirical research, to be effective. This interpretation can be seen clearly in practice in the USA where research into aspects of pedagogy has been more prolific than here. In England perhaps the most obvious use is in the various micro-teaching programmes which have been implemented in recent years by a number of higher education institutions. For example, Butterworth (1989) describes a micro-teaching programme for PE students and their reactions to it. It involves the identification of a number of specific strategies which are seen to be central to 'good teaching' and discussion subsequent to a lesson (which maybe taught to a small group, to a whole class for a short time or to a whole class for a whole lesson) about the student's success or otherwise of putting these strategies into action. In many cases the lesson is videotaped for later analysis.

Feedback from students participating in such programmes has been positive and it seems to be seen as a valuable learning experience. The key feature of these kinds of exercises is that they take as their main focus the achievement of the learning task with little attention to the context in which that learning is taking place or to the content itself. Clearly, for the student teacher, this kind of reflection, which helps them to acquire basic teaching competences can be useful. What it does not address is whether the competence they are acquiring is actually valuable and helping pupils to learn in the way anticipated or assumed. For example, a micro-teaching programme might help students to become very efficient and effective in presenting a specific practice to a group of pupils but the practice itself could actually be a poor way of learning that particular skill and a different activity altogether might be more effective for the pupils.

An alternative approach sees reflection as a form of deliberation among competing views of teaching, that is, the consideration of educational events in practice. Research knowledge in this context is used not to direct practice but to inform it and to help to understand it. There is a belief that in reflecting about particular events in context, one deliberates between and among competing views of teaching and examines each in the light of the consequences of the action it entails. The work on teaching styles by Mosston (Mosston and Ashworth, 1986) discussed in Chapter 4, provides an example of this kind of reflection. Mosston's work considers the relationship between specific teaching styles and learning outcomes other than the purely physical. Active involvement of pupils in decision-making increases as one moves through Mosston's spectrum and likely learning outcomes change, thereby raising many questions about relative priorities in the learning process.

For example, Mosston describes 'reciprocal' teaching as one where pupils work in pairs with one playing the teacher role and as a style which emphasises personal and social skills as well as physical performance. For some teachers, the time spent talking through the requirements for helping a peer effectively is seen as time taken away from practising physical skills and as a result they reject this style. For others, the personal and social benefits which accrue far outweigh any loss in performance should this occur. They would argue that short term loss would, anyway, be made up over a period of time. For the student then, this kind of reflection involves weighing up the advantages and disadvantages of adopting particular approaches before making decisions about what style or strategy to adopt. If the student is to be able to engage effectively in this kind of reflection, the school and the department need to be sufficiently flexible to accept the use of an approach or a teaching style which might not have been their choice. Clearly a balance has to be struck between allowing complete carte blanche which could jeopardise the learning of the pupils and forcing students into a straitjacket of existing departmental practice which may not enable them to develop their own style.

A third perspective sees reflection as something where sources of knowledge are found in both the action setting, that is, the gymnasium or playing field, and in the practical application of personal knowledge. Situations need to be recast once they have been clarified, rethinking the assumptions upon which initial understandings of a problematic issue were based, prior to reconsideration of the range of responses that might be used. This demands consideration of the situational and institutional contexts of teaching. An example of an issue which may or may not be viewed as problematic is related to equal opportunities in relation to gender. Initial teacher education courses have now become mixed sex after many years of single sex provision and there is a significant amount of mixed sex PE teaching in secondary schools. At one stage, the curriculum offered to male and female students was viewed as unproblematic. Male students followed courses in the teaching of rugby and soccer and female students parallel courses in the teaching of hockey and netball on the basis of perceived needs of the schools in which the students were likely to find future employment. Female students followed courses in the teaching of dance while male students did not. An alternative view has emerged which sees differentiation of the curriculum along gender lines as problematic and which looks for ways of mitigating its effects. This may be through offering all activities to everyone or through offering options in such a way that students are challenged to make decisions rather than to assume that their most appropriate choice is a traditionally 'male' or 'female' activity.

Similar decisions have to be taken at the school level in planning the curriculum through a particular Key Stage. Advocates of this interpretation of reflection would argue that seeing curriculum content as problematic is important. There is a great deal of evidence that physical education is seen positively by some pupils and negatively by others and that its content and teaching methodology tends to reinforce certain social values which some would wish to question. For example, as Tinning (1991) points out, the message often given is that one can only succeed in a competitive environment if there is a loser, that girls are inferior to boys in matters physical and that the slim mesomorph is the only acceptable body shape. The extent to which these messages are given varies enormously from school to school at present. This is clearly reflection at a policy level rather than part of day to day practice.

Reflective teaching can therefore be interpreted in different ways. These approaches are summarised by Hellison and Templin (1991). Table 2.1 is based upon their summary.

For the student, survival and the demonstration of professional competence is, understandably, likely to be a higher priority than reflection on a range of curriculum and educational issues, some of which might, more properly, be seen as the province of further professional development to be undertaken at a later stage in a teaching career. Nevertheless, choices to support, for example particular views, such as a competitive orthodoxy or curriculum negotiation, should be made as conscious decisions having thought about the alternatives, rather than decisions taken by default.

What kind of teacher training?

The process model applies both to the student teacher and to the school pupil as learners.

Table 2.1 A continuum of conceptualisations of reflective practice

Conceptualisation	*Examples*	*Context*
Analysis of teaching strategies	Clarity of questioning techniques Criteria for effective demonstrations	Practice
Assumptions and consequences of the teaching act	Reciprocal teaching for personal and social education Practice style for improvement in skill	Practice
Values and goals	Promotion of health and fitness rather than a competitive ethos	Policy and practice
Ethical, social and political issues	How to implement an anti-racist policy	Policy and practice

The National Curriculum Attainment Target for Physical Education involves planning performing and evaluating with the major emphasis on performance. This plan, do, review cycle is fundamental to the learning which is necessary if pupils are to leave school with the skills, knowledge and understanding to be independently active. The process model is a cyclical model within which smaller cycles operate as illustrated in Figures 2.1 and 2.1a, b and c.

The student teacher needs to plan, teach and review just as the school pupil is taught through the plan, perform, evaluate model (Chapter 3).

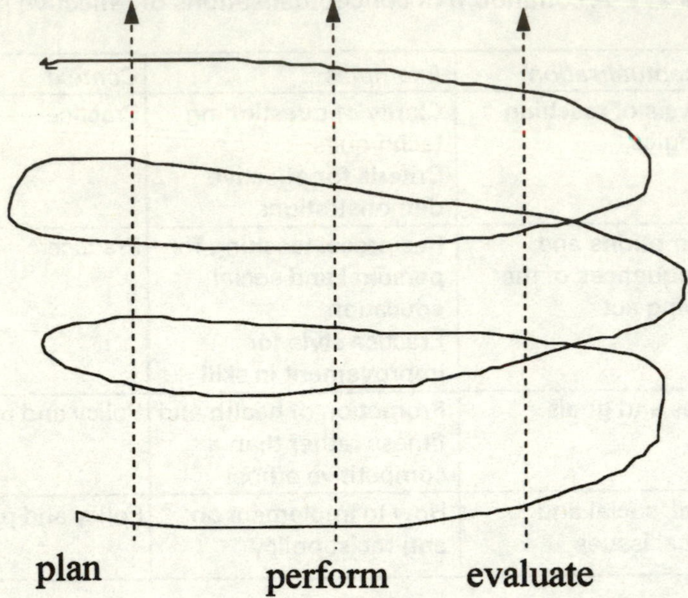

Figure 2.1

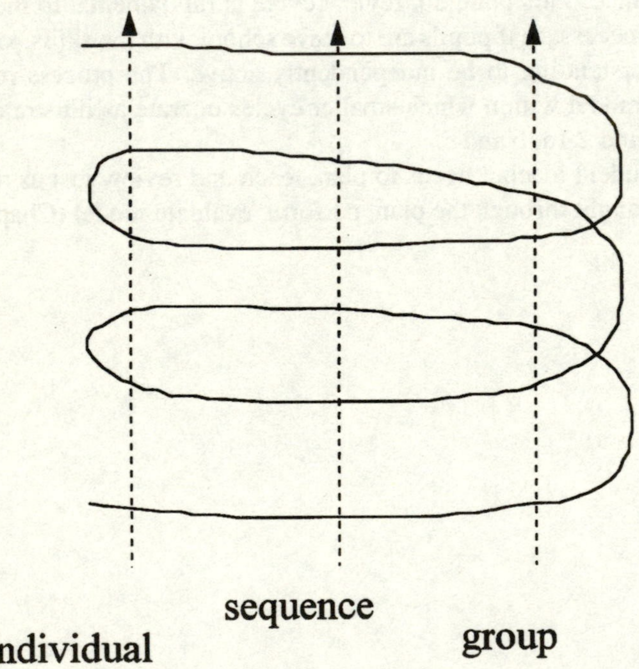

Figure 2.1a Planning

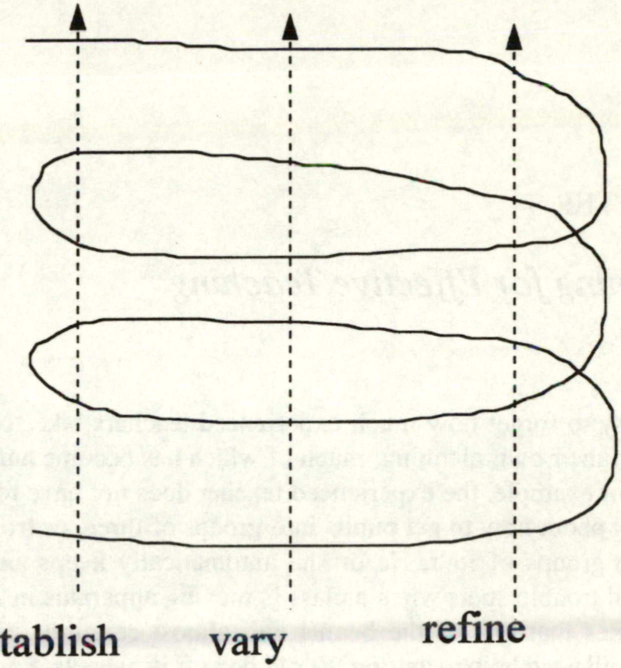

Figure 2.1b Performance

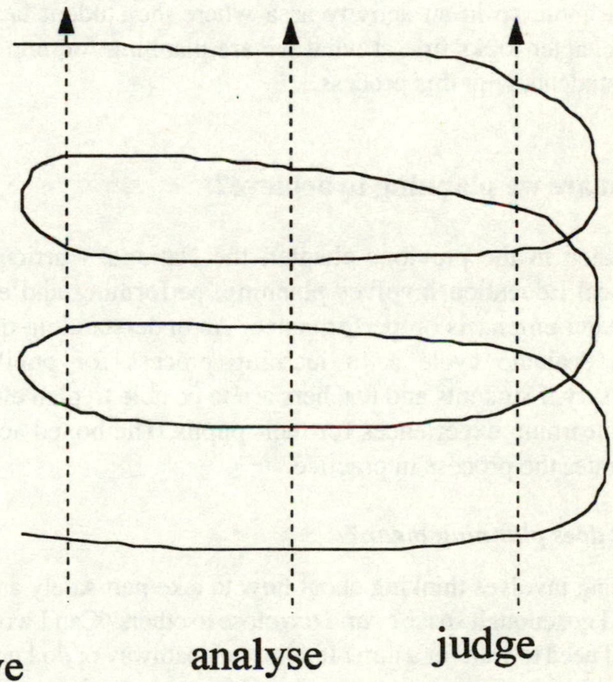

Figure 2.1c Evaluation

CHAPTER 3

Planning for Effective Teaching

It is easy to forget how much experienced teachers take for granted in terms of their own planning, much of which has become automatic over time. For example, the experienced teacher does not have to spend time thinking about how to get pupils into groups of three, or from groups of three to groups of four. He or she automatically keeps an eye on the potential trouble spots when a class is moving apparatus in the gym and anticipates that one of the beams will almost certainly stick and that pupils will need help in getting the old box off its wheels. For the student, careful planning of all aspects of the lesson is essential if things are to go smoothly. The actual teaching content will also need detailed planning, all the more so in an activity area where the student lacks experience. This chapter looks first at what we are planning for, and then at how to help students with this process.

What are we planning to achieve?

As stated in the previous chapter, the National Curriculum Order for Physical Education involves planning, performing and evaluating with the major emphasis on performance. An understanding of the plan, perform, evaluate cycle as a learning process for pupils is therefore necessary if students and teachers are to be able to plan effective and relevant learning experiences for their pupils. The boxed account opposite illustrates the process in practice.

What does planning mean?

Planning involves thinking about how to take part safely and purposefully. Have I got enough space? Am I too close to others? Can I work continuously or do I need to wait for a turn? It this a safe pathway or do I need to choose an alternative? Is the mat correctly placed for me to perform this vault?

[PLAN—PERFORM—EVALUATE]

Sukbir arrives at secondary school with a limited range of securely learned skills in gymnastics and games and the ability to observe and describe perceptively. He is able to plan his work in order to share space and equipment effectively, to compose simple sequences in gymnastics and to use basic games skills in a games context provided he is not put under too much pressure. By the end of Year 7 Sukbir is able to plan a gymnastics apparatus sequence using box, bench and four mats so that he can perform his piece of work at the same time as three other pupils and so that certain prescribed actions are included. He is able to watch the performance of others and describe it accurately in terms of the skills and actions included. He can now swim a considerable distance in his chosen stroke and 25 metres in two other strokes, albeit with difficulty. He can now use soccer skills in games and under some pressure and has learned a new range of basketball skills, some of which he can apply in a game.

By the end of Year 9 Sukbir is able to contribute to the planning of a group sequence including advanced partner balance skills and a combination of canon and unison work. He has learned a number of advanced apparatus skills. He can draw up criteria by which he will 'assess' the work of other groups and can apply these in practice. He can use his swimming strokes in survival situations involving swimming some distance in clothing and can plan a strategy for saving someone in difficulties in deep open water. He can play an effective game of soccer and basketball and is developing tactical skills in badminton. He can observe others' play and make constructive comment on the success or otherwise of tactics used. He has joined a local leisure centre in order to swim and play badminton.

Planning involves tactical and strategic planning in the games context. It involves composing/choreographing in gymnastics or dance.

Planning involves planning training schedules for health and fitness or for participation in activities such as swimming or athletics. It involves planning safe routes in OAA (outdoor and adventurous activities).

Planning involves thinking about how best to perform a skill successfully, particularly during the learning phase. Where do I position my feet in order to stand up at the end of a forward roll? Where should the follow through go if the chest pass is to be successful? How should I hold the racket in order to perform an effective backhand drive?

The language of planning includes analysis, exploration, selection, formulation – all leading to implementation.

What does performing mean?

Performing involves the skills, knowledge and understanding needed to take part in a range of physical activities.

It includes performance of single actions or skills – forward roll, front somersault, chest pass, forehand drive, breast stroke leg kick, etc.

It includes the performance of these skills under pressure in the games situation and the choice of the appropriate skill for a specific context – a high clear in badminton to force the opponent onto the defensive, a dig in volleyball where the ball is too low to set.

It includes the performance of these skills in a sequence in gymnastics or dance and the ability to perform increasingly complex sequences. These can also involve work with a partner or in a group.

It involves the ability to conform to rules or conventions.

It involves the ability to sustain performance over a period of time – running a distance, practising a skill.

It involves being able to refine skills through practice or rehearsal.

It involves the ability to adapt to new situations – playing a different position in a game or with different people, reacting to changing weather conditions when sailing.

It involves understanding the principles of effective performance in order to sustain a high level of expertise.

It involves the demonstration of skill and expertise.

Performance evolves through establishing skills or movement patterns, adapting, refining or varying them, and improvisation.

What does evaluating involve?

Evaluating involves making judgements about one's own performance or that of others which will help in future planning and performance.

It involves making simple judgements about performance against given criteria – were his feet together? did she kick the ball with the inside of her foot?

It involves recognising others' success – how many baskets did your partner score? how many sit ups did your partner manage? how many widths did your partner swim?

It involves making judgements about performances against given criteria – were there three balances in that sequence and what linking actions were used? how successful was the group in synchronising their actions?

It involves making judgements about safe practice – is that apparatus too close to the wall? is it safe to use those two grids for different games? what clothing should we take on this walk?

It involves making comparisons about performance – who got most height off the trampette, why do you think that was? whose shot has the greater power? why?

It involves monitoring and adjusting one's own performance – if I stand up on the other foot I will be in a better position to do the cartwheel; I need to turn my shoulder further to get the direction of the pass accurate.

It involves analysing performance against criteria which are at least partly identified by the pupil.

It involves identifying the key aspects of a performance which need further practice or key areas of weakness in a game.

Evaluation requires observation, description and analysis, comparison and making judgements.

Progression in the three elements of the process model is summarised in Table 3.1.

Why is planning important?

It is easy to characterise higher education as more concerned with the appearance of the lesson plan than with what actually goes on in the gymnasium or on the playing field and the school as custodian of the practical 'real' world. The reality is that all concerned with the student's learning should see the interaction between student and pupils and the quality of the learning which the student promotes as the priority while recognising that, for most students, detailed planning is an essential prerequisite for successful teaching.

Table 3.1 Summary of progression

Dimension	*Content*	*Context*	*Process*
Plan	for individual actions – short phrases – complex sequences simple strategies – complex tactics	alone – pairs – groups with a partner small side games – full size games	analyse, explore, select, formulate, carry out
Perform	simple single actions – technically demanding single actions single actions – complex sequences static or slow motion skills – full speed skills unopposed skills – opposed skills limited range of actions/ skills – wide repertoire of actions/skills basic competence – refined performance	alone – pairs – groups with a partner – small side games – full size games	establish, adapt, refine, vary, improvise
Evaluate	simple movements – short phrases or game episodes – complex sequences or games	given criteria – negotiated criteria – self chosen criteria	observe, describe, analyse, compare, make judgements

It also has to be remembered that, for the student, the file of lesson plans is part of the evidence which he or she will present of competence to teach, particularly of the DFE competence statement which requires all newly qualified teachers to 'produce coherent lesson plans which take account of NCATs and of the schools' curriculum policies' (DFE, 1992). This evidence constitutes part of the formal assessment of most courses. It is required by external examiners who are required to satisfy themselves that standards are consistent with those elsewhere. It may be required by senior management within the school who wish to confirm that student progress is satisfactory. It will certainly be scrutinised by OFSTED in the course of inspecting initial teacher training courses and probably during the course of school OFSTED inspections where these coincide with student placements. Depending upon how the responsibility for the student has been shared between the higher education institution and the school, the university tutor may need to see plans as evidence that the student has done the preparation necessary to begin their placement. Above all though, plans are an aid for the student and a record of what they have taught, which have the potential to serve as a valuable resource for them in the future.

Some specific objectives for planning

We ask students to plan their lessons for various reasons.

- *Plans as articulation of thinking*. In many instances the process of thinking through exactly what is planned for a particular phase in a specific lesson is as important as the actual writing it down. The process of writing down may well prompt thought about other issues which need to be addressed. For example, seeing 'groups of 2, groups of 3, groups of 5' written against different practices may prompt the student to consider how the pupils are going to be organised into these different groups and whether this amount of reorganisation during one lesson is necessary or desirable.
- *Plans as evidence of preparation*. Student teachers are given the responsibility for teaching classes normally taken by a qualified teacher. The teacher remains accountable, at the end of the day, for the achievements of the pupils. It is therefore reasonable for the teacher to have evidence of adequate preparation. While this may also be provided by talking to the student, a written plan can show quickly and simply whether likely eventualities have been planned for. As already mentioned, there are also various others with a legitimate interest in the quality of the student's planning.
- *Plans as a basis for discussion and evaluation*. Many of the questions in the following section (*Talking about lesson plans*) are matters which the experienced teacher addresses without conscious thought but which the beginning teacher needs to consider and think through. Talking some of these through with the student can help the experienced teacher to articulate aspects of their own practice and thereby help the student to anticipate issues which will arise during the course of a lesson. The lesson plan is a useful starting point which will give the mentor some indication of the extent to which the student has thought through these questions.
- *Plans for survival*. While experienced teachers can think through what they are going to teach as they drive to school in the car or as they walk down the corridor, drawing on a bank of previous successful lessons, the student does not have recourse to such experience and knowledge. In the early days of learning to teach, planning is often a necessary survival tool if disaster is not to ensue. It is important that experienced

teachers recognise this and expect student teachers to need to plan. While the mentor will almost certainly appreciate this, it is a message which also needs to be reinforced by other members of the department.

What should plans include?

There is no 'right' way to write a unit of work or lesson plan, although most partnerships provide proformas which ensure that essential elements are addressed. An example of a proforma for both a unit of work and a lesson plan are given in Figures 3.1 and 3.2.

Most students find it easier to plan for performance related objectives than for planning and evaluation or for wider issues such as health or personal and social aims. Even if these appear as an objective at the top of a lesson plan, there may be nothing to suggest how they are to be achieved during the course of the lesson. For example, co-operating in groups may be an aim for a lesson but the student may assume that this will happen simply by organising pupils into groups. If there is no real co-operation during the lesson, the student may assume that the pupils are simply not capable of working together. They may need help in thinking through strategies which they might use to actively foster co-operative work, such as including some discussion with pupils of behaviours conducive to successful group work. These strategies then need to be included in their plans.

Talking about lesson plans

This section looks at the issues which all should address and suggests questions which the mentor should ask of the student if the answer is not clear from the plan.

1. *What are the pupils going to learn?*

This generally appears on plans as

- aims
- objectives
- learning outcomes.

These may be

- physical (related to planning, performing, evaluating)
- health related
- safety related
- related to personal or social education.

It is generally helpful to encourage students to think about what they expect the pupils to be able to do or to know by the end of the lesson, and to write this down in terms of the pupils' learning rather than the student's teaching.

Questions to ask

What do you intend the pupils to learn?
Is this a new skill?
Revision of an old one?
Further development of one previously learned?
What assumptions are you making about the pupils' knowledge or abilities?
How does it relate to National Curriculum requirements?

2. *What tasks are going to be set during the course of the lesson and in what order?*

This generally appears on plans as

material
task
learning activity.

For some students during the early stages of learning to teach it will be necessary to write tasks down verbatim or at least think through their wording in some detail.

Questions to ask

How do you expect pupils to react to the task?
Does the task cater for all abilities? What will you expect from the most able, from the least able?
What will you do if the task proves too difficult? too easy?
What difficulties do you anticipate?
How do you envisage helping pupils to improve?

3. *How will the student help pupils to answer the task?*

This generally appears on plans as

teaching points
assessment pointers
teaching activities
teaching and assessment strategy.

It will involve thinking about *how* to help pupils. A common problem is that students tell pupils *what* to do rather than how to do it. Thus they may say:

'Jump higher' rather than 'Push off more strongly' or 'Swing your arms to help you to get higher', or

'Make your pass accurate' rather than 'Look for where your team mate will be and aim the ball there' or 'Turn your shoulders further so that your pass reaches the player'.

It also involves thinking about what teaching style should be used and about how assessment of pupil performance will inform the next stage in the teaching process.

PHYSICAL EDUCATION

SCHEME OF WORK

ACTIVITY .... YEAR .... NO. OF WEEKS .....

LESSON LENGTH .... NO. OF PUPILS....... M/F/MIXED............

LOCATION..

PREVIOUS EXPERIENCE ....

AIMS

NATIONAL CURRICULUM PoS - GENERAL + NATIONAL CURRICULUM GENERAL REQUIREMENT

ACTIVITY SPECIFIC PoS

OTHER LEARNING OUTCOMES (IT, Language, Problem-solving, Health, PSE, Equal Opportunities, etc)

Figure 3.1

DETAILS OF SCHEME

ORDER*	LEARNING ACTIVITIES			LEARNING OUTCOMES
	PLAN	PERFORM	EVALUATE	

*Use this column to indicate the order in which you plan to introduce the learning activities. The numbers may correspond to the weeks of the course, but you should not try to predict precisely what you will cover each week at this stage.

LESSON PLAN – PHYSICAL EDUCATION

Activity: NET/RACKET GAMES – Volleyball | Class: YEAR 8 | Date: Nov 1994

Lesson length: 50 minutes | No. of pupils: 30 | Location: GYM

Learning and assessment focus:

To appreciate the need for teamwork
To develop co-operative questions
To develop communication skills
To understand and use the dig and volley to create opportunity for attacking shots

Time	Learning Activity	Teaching and Assessment Strategy (e.g. teaching points, teaching styles) (including alternatives for less able and more able)	Organisation	Resources
10 mins	Intro/Warm up	Pupils move immediately into known	Groups of 3	
	– dig + volley drill	practice	volley	Selection of volleyballs
		Pupil organised – choose preferred	xx xx shot	Mini-volleyballs
		ball	and follow	Sponge balls
	– stretching	Pupil led – each group member	dig	Stretching
		leads other two in one stretch	Groups of 3	Workcards
30 mins		Focus (1) – team work	. . . .	String
		Set challenge: team to work together to	. ______________ .	Volleyballs
		get ball set up at net	. . . .	Markers
		Ability conditions:	string net down centre of gym	
		1) – 3 touch, no bounce	5 courts using markers	
		2) – 4 touch, one initial bounce	Group of 6 on each court	
		3) – 5 touch, ball can bounce once after each touch	Teacher moves around outside of courts – observe, question, assist	
		Questioning each group – where best to stand on court – how best to get ball set up at net		
		Whole group review – need to communicate – all put ideas in, all listen – need to co-operate – try out all good ideas – carry out given role		
	game ↕ practice ↙ ↘ technique group drill	Focus (2) – shots to set ball up at net Volley when ball high Dig when ball low Aim to work ball towards the 'setter' Problem solving – direct reciprocal teaching teaching	Games of 3 v 3 Teacher observes performance Assisting groups where necessary Groups help each other with practices or reciprocal testing tasks	Practice workcards Reciprocal workcards
10 mins	Group review	Teacher concludes – highlight – communication – co-operation – positions on court – use of available touches – choice of shot – where to next? Smash?		

Figure 3.2

Questions to ask

Which teaching styles will you use? Why are these appropriate?
Do you plan to demonstrate?
You or a pupil?
How will it be organised?
What will you want to emphasise for the observers?
What questions might you ask?
What do you expect from the pupils?
What do you expect to have to say to help them?

4. *What organisational issues are there?*

As effective organisation and management of the lesson are prerequisites for successful teaching, these issues are crucial for the student and can be areas which are taken for granted. This is especially so if the student has observed good teaching where everything seems to happen very easily without realising just how much expertise in organisation underpins the lesson.

Questions to ask

What size groups are needed?

This question has to be considered in the context of other factors. It may be that groups of two would be ideal for maximum activity and involvement of all pupils all the time but there may not be enough equipment (e.g. for a ball between two) or there may not be enough space for sixteen pairs to work safely (e.g. practising hockey passes in a restricted indoor space). On the other hand, during a warm up in a sports hall or outside, there should be no reason for large groups taking turns with the standing waiting which this involves.

How are pupils going to get into groups of this size?

Are pupils going to select their own groups or will the teacher decide? Sometimes there is a conflict here between the aim of encouraging independent behaviour best achieved by giving pupils the responsibility of organising themselves and the aim of enhancing all pupils' self esteem which will not be achieved by standing conspicuously as the last pupil to be chosen.

Will they be mixed or single sex?

It is arguable whether forcing pupils to work with others of the opposite sex against their will is a sensible way of organising groups or of maximising learning. Decisions here need to be made taking account of the make up of individual classes and of the kinds of work involved. For example if groups of five or six are simply sharing the same working space such as a grid in games or an apparatus arrangement in the gym, then mixed sex groups may be quite feasible. If more interaction and co-operative working is needed then it may be more productive to allow pupils to be organised in single sex groups. An example of this was given by a student who had a Year 9 mixed sex basketball group. She had organised mixed sex teams, believing that this was in the interest of equal opportunities and pupil learning but was becoming frustrated by the reluctance of pupils of either sex to pass to someone of the opposite sex. The result was a game where finding someone free and in a space became secondary to finding someone of the same sex to pass to even if the result was an interception or other loss of possession. The next week the girls asked whether they could play together against the boys. Although the student was concerned, assuming that they would be beaten comfortably, the girls argued forcefully that they had different skills and if they could play together they would give the boys a run for their money. The student eventually agreed to try this arrangement. The girls used their superior passing skills and the shooting skills of two of their team while the boys dribbled the ball much more and all wanted to score baskets. The outcome was victory for the girls and an excellent example of capitalising upon one's strengths.

Do members need to be similar height/size?

This is an issue in some games situations, e.g. rugby where scrums of different sizes can be dangerous. It may be an issue, e.g. in gymnastics, where similar size groups can enable apparatus such as beams or boxes to be adjusted to suit different groups.

Are groups of several different sizes used during the lesson? Is this necessary? What are the organisational implications?

A mistake sometimes made by inexperienced teachers or those whose experience has been in working with advanced or adult groups is to organise practices all requiring different group sizes. The result can be that more time is spent getting into and out of groups than in practical work.

Is there enough space for the activities which are being planned?

What safety issues might arise?

Will all pupils be able to work at once? If not what will you do?

What equipment is needed? Does it all work, e.g. are the basketballs all blown up or are several flat at the back of a cupboard?

Can the student work it? Does he or she know how the cassette recorder works? Do the numbers work? Can he or she operate the beams safely and correctly?

What will happen to equipment no longer needed, e.g. spare balls? Is it safe to leave them at the side of the playing area or do they need to be put elsewhere?

Time?

How long should each teaching episode take?

What will be omitted if time gets short?
Students frequently simply work through their lesson plan in the order in which it is written. This can mean that the consequence of early mistakes on the part of the student can mean no game for the pupils or no apparatus or no compositional work in dance. Prioritising tasks earlier in the lesson and planning to leave one or two out if necessary will help to ensure that lessons do not become distorted and pupil learning is not put at risk.

5. *How will you assess pupil learning?*
This is inextricably linked with clear learning outcomes. See Chapter 6 for further discussion of pupil assessment.

Aspects of planning

The production of units of work and individual lesson plans are a normal requirement for all student teachers and examples of proformas which may be used to help with this process have already been given. There are however other aspects of planning, taken for granted by experienced teachers, which may well be necessary for the student teacher. Thinking around aspects of planning in a way which helps the students to put the content of a specific lesson in a context is needed if the student is to have the understanding and confidence to be flexible in his or her teaching. For example, lesson content is always a selection of what is possible. In activity areas with which the student is relatively unfamiliar, appreciation of where the content of a specific lesson fits into a larger area of work may be helped by a content analysis. This involves going through all the possible aspects of work which might be covered so that the student is able to make a selection from a range of possibilities rather than being limited to his or her restricted knowledge or experience.

Planning for differentiation

If all pupils are to learn effectively, then differentiation is important although demanding. As a starting point students can be encouraged to think of planning for groups of pupils with similar abilities and aptitudes.

These are just three of the pupils which we might find in any Key Stage 3 class. How do we cater for all of them bearing in mind that they all need success and challenge?

Given the potential material contained within the Key Stage 3 Programme of Study, the teacher has plenty of choice and there is absolutely no need to impose the same content upon every child. Differentiation can be achieved through a number of strategies, some of which are used routinely by teachers who may not be fully aware of the differentiation potential offered.

Ramela is 13 and until about 18 months ago was an enthusiastic and accomplished participant. At puberty she grew several inches and put on a significant amount of weight. She no longer has sufficient upper body strength to support her weight easily on her hands. She finds her gymnastics lessons frustrating and now opts out whenever possible. In games she feels awkward alongside her less mature or slimmer peers and avoids involvement when she can.

Tracy is also 13 and has yet to reach puberty. She is slight and lightweight. She is very flexible but lacks strength although, because of her light weight and petite build, many gymnastics skills come easily. She is also a quick and skilful netball player who could make the county squad if she trained. She will practise willingly and learn new skills, but resists any suggestion that she should try to improve her strength because she 'doesn't want to grow all fat and muscly'.

Mark is 13 and physically mature. He goes to weight training at the local leisure centre and has excellent upper body strength. He enjoys strength based activities such as rope or beam work and also vaulting. He is also a good all round games player. He thinks floor work is very boring and regularly misses the apparatus part of the lesson because of earlier misdemeanours. He also dislikes practising in games and often fails to complete the lesson as a result.

Differentiation is often described as being by task or by outcome. Differentiation by task means setting a range of tasks appropriate for either different individuals or different groups of pupils. For example, a class could be divided into three groups for a swimming lesson. The non-swimmers would be set a completely different task from the more able swimmers who would be working on a different stroke from the middle ability group. A gymnastics class could be set five different tasks on five different apparatus arrangements, with the pupils allowed to choose which task to answer, subject to there being no more than a specified number working at one apparatus station. Given the differences illustrated by the three pupil cameos above, differentiation by outcome, through which the same task is set to all, but with a range of acceptable outcomes, may be less successful than differentiation by task. This is with the proviso that the latter should be used for offering choice and not simply in a way which highlights ability differences. Certainly it should be possible for pupils to have some choice in the way they progress work over a series of lessons.

Differentiation through content

This may operate within activities or may involve choice between activities. Within a specific theme in gymnastics, for example symmetry, or within a specific action category, for example, rolling, different pupils may work within a different content emphasis. Within the context of symmetry, some pupils might be attempting a variety of symmetrical balances while others might be trying different flight activities with a symmetrical body position. In the context of rolling, some pupils might be learning a circle roll, others a fish roll, others a backward roll to straddle. Within the games activity area, there could well be scope for pupils to have some choice within a games category by the end of Key Stage 3. For example, pupils could be offered four team games and invited to opt for units of work in two of them. By Key Stage 4 differentiation by content is usually offered through provision of activity options.

Differentiation through pace

In the context of physical education, the pace at which pupils perform or practise may well be a function of physical fitness and capacity as well as cognition or concentration. For example, some pupils may only be able to sustain activities which involve taking the weight on the hands for a short period, whereas others may be able to sustain such activity for a long time. Use of workcards which enable pupils to move on when they have finished the tasks on one, can provide opportunities for all to be challenged at their own pace.

In swimming some pupils will be capable of sustained stroke practice while others will need to rest briefly at the end of a width or a length before attempting another. In games some pupils will need to practise either stationary or at a slow pace in order to improve a skill while others will be capable of practising the same skill at full speed or against opposition.

Differentiation through level

This may be related to differentiation through pace. Where workcards are progressive, perhaps through setting increasingly difficult or more complex tasks, pupils may be working at different levels as well as at a pace appropriate to their abilities. In the games context, games of different sizes can be played or some groups may play a small game with teams of the same size while others may practise with a large attacking team against a small number of defenders.

Differentiation through access

In order for all pupils to have access to particular activities it may be necessary to modify the presentation for some. Some pupils will only be able to attempt some skills if physical support is available, either for safety or for confidence. Some pupils may have very particular needs, such as brightly coloured benches or balls which give an audible signal to help the visually impaired pupil.

Differentiation through sequence

While some skills have certain prerequisites, for example the ability to support the weight on the hands before attempting to learn a handspring, others may be attempted in any order. Pupils can be given apparatus choices so that they choose whether to develop skills of balancing using a beam, or hanging and swinging using ropes, or flight using a box. Some pupils may find one swimming stroke much easier to master than another and will make more progress if they are able to gain proficiency in their preferred stroke before attempting another one.

Differentiation through teaching style

Good teachers use a range of teaching styles and strategies without necessarily thinking of their use as a form of differentiation. Pupils however often respond differently to different approaches, some of which will match individual's preferred learning styles better than others.

Differentiation through interest

Particularly at Key Stage 4 or the latter stages of Key Stage 3, lesson content may be negotiated to reflect pupil interests.

Differentiation through pupil groupings

Pupils often work in friendship groups, however this form of grouping may not be the most appropriate for all work. Do pupils need to be split by size, e.g. for scrummaging in rugby? Do pupils need to be split by ability, e.g. in swimming to keep non-swimmers in shallow water? Are group or individual activities more effective in catering for individual differences? Grouping according to a combination of size and ability may enable gymnastics apparatus to be put at different heights to accommodate all. In some contexts, allowing pupils to choose whether they work alone, in pairs or in larger groups may also accommodate individual differences and preferences.

Differentiation through resources

This form of differentiation can be provided in various ways. Do all pupils have the same resources or is there potential for some variation dependent upon ability? In the gymnasium do all boxes or beams have to be at the same height? Can pupils choose their own apparatus? In games does every game have to be played with the same implements or equipment? Can different sizes/weights of ball be used? In the swimming pool are all pupils asked to do the same or are some provided with floats/armbands or other aids?

Planning for progression

Progression should be evident both within a lesson and through a series of lessons. Figure 2.1 in Chapter 2 outlines some of the dimensions of progression in relation to planning, performing and evaluating. Understanding of progression is linked to understanding of what it is that pupils are to learn. Asking students to focus upon what pupils are learning rather than on what they are doing, from an early stage in their training, will help them to appreciate this.

Jane and Michael were given a small group of able 11 year olds for a gymnastics lesson. At the end, they were thrilled with what the children had been able to do and enthusiastic about their commitment and involvement in all the tasks which they had been set. Their mentor shared their enjoyment of the lesson and then asked them what they thought they had taught the children. They named a string of skills. The mentor asked how they knew that the children had been learning rather than simply reproducing these skills. There was a silence.... A lesson had been learned.

Progression can be in the difficulty of the tasks achieved, in the quality of the response and in the context in which it is produced.

Have pupils extended their personal repertoire? This means increasing the range of actions and skills which the pupil can perform. It may mean acquiring new skills – a handstand or a circle roll in gymnastics, a flick pass in hockey, the butterfly in swimming. It may mean extending the repertoire through adding different dimensions – ending a forward roll in many different ways, using a jump shot against stronger opposition or under increased time pressure, swimming in clothes as a survival exercise.

Have pupils learned new actions, skills, sequences or tactics which are technically more difficult for them? This is about the need for personal challenge. For one pupil it may mean learning to stand up from a forward roll without using his or her hands. For another it may mean lifting into a handstand off two feet with straight legs. For a third it may involve passing the ball on the move when being closely marked. For a fourth it could entail mastering a specific sequence of passes in a tactical move.

Has quality of performance developed? This is particularly applicable in gymnastics and dance. Initially clarity of body shape and body tension may only be achieved in held positions. Progression is shown where the same clarity and tension is present throughout the performance of first single actions, then parts of sequences and finally, through whole performances. In other activity areas it could be applied to refining stroke technique in swimming or in a racket game.

Have pupils succeeded in integrating actions into increasingly complex sequences or into tactical strategies? Progression in sequence work may involve creating and sustaining quality performance through longer sequences; performing sequences using first simple and then complex apparatus; performing sequences in pairs, trios or larger groups; incorporating added dimensions such as varied pathways, different levels, changes of speed (all introduced at Key Stage 2). Tactical progression might involve moving from being able to contribute to a simple series of moves in a small group with limited opposition to demonstrating the ability to work as part of a complex tactical strategy involving many players and with full opposition. It might involve coping in a 3 v 3 situation rather than with a 3 v 1.

Planning over a period of time will be informed by the outcome of the previous lesson. Lesson evaluation thus becomes a key part of the planning cycle. The suggestions given in Chapter 10 for mentor observation of lessons can also be used by students to evaluate their own teaching.

CHAPTER 4

Teaching Styles

Circular 9/92 states that NQTs should be able to employ a range of teaching strategies and that they should be able to decide when teaching the whole class, groups, pairs or individuals is appropriate for particular learning purposes. Strategies and styles are terms used in different ways by different people. For the purposes of this book, style is used to refer to a general approach within which other more specific strategies might be employed. This chapter and the following will look at both.

A number of different writers have, at various times, identified different teaching styles and related them to particular philosophies of teaching or to specific learning outcomes. All define these teaching approaches in terms of the extent to which pupils are involved in the learning process. Bilbrough and Jones (1973) described approaches to gymnastics teaching as 'direct', 'limitation' or 'indirect'. Kane (Schools Council, 1974) in a large scale study of physical education teaching used the categories 'direct', 'guided discovery', 'individual', 'problem solving' and 'creative'. The most detailed analysis of teaching styles is that undertaken by Mosston and Ashworth (1986) who describe a spectrum of teaching styles in terms of the extent to which decisions are taken by pupil or teacher. Although this work is open to criticism, not least for ignoring the context of learning and factors such as teacher expectations, it has become the most widely used framework in both initial and in-service training in this country over recent years. Student teachers need an appreciation of the range of styles available to them if they are to maximise learning opportunities for all pupils. This is not least because pupils learn in different ways. Although there is relatively little written about pupil learning styles, it does seem clear that learning is more effective if the teaching style used is consistent with the preferred learning style of the pupil and that a mismatch will have an adverse effect on learning.

The following description of the various styles is based upon a broad interpretation of Mosston's definitions and indicates ways in which pupil involvement in learning can be increased even within styles which give most of the decision-making to the teacher. It is followed by some suggestions for student activities to increase awareness of different styles and to help them to see different styles in action. As indicated in Chapter 6 and in Activity C at the end of this chapter, teaching styles could well be a focus of lesson debriefs.

Style	*Characteristics*	*Outcomes*
Style A Command	Teacher takes decisions. Pupils are expected to follow instructions and perform. Immediate response. Large amount of time on task and for repetition. No allowance for individual differences.	Conformity. Uniform behaviour. Potential for high levels of activity. Safe learning of high risk activities and therefore, confidence. Accurate replication of a motif or action or of a part of either.

This style can be seen in a variety of activity contexts. Maybe the most obvious example is in the typical aerobics class which displays all the attributes of the Command Style. Pupils follow instructions, respond as a class, conform in their response, achieve high levels of activity and numerous repetitions of the various exercises. It can also be seen in the teaching of high risk activities where the teacher takes all decisions in the interests of safety. For example in trampolining, where pupils are learning somersaults with teacher support, the teacher will not only tell the pupil exactly what to do, but will also dictate the timing through counting the performer in to the move. The same procedures will be used in teaching some vaulting activities. Synchronised swimming is a further example of an activity in which a command style may be used when choreographing a routine with a group of pupils. It may be used to teach a simple motif in dance which is subsequently developed by pupils using different styles.

When to use it?

When conformity is required.
When a high level of activity is a priority.
When safety is paramount.

Examples of tasks

1. Pupils are told to attempt a front somersault on the trampoline on a count of three so that the teacher can support them.
2. Pupils are asked to watch a short dance motif and then to copy it as the teacher repeats it.

Style	*Characteristics*	*Outcomes*
Style B Practice	Teacher takes most decisions. Pupils take some decisions about, e.g. location, timing, pace. Teacher has time to give individual feedback. Pupils are able to work individually at their own pace.	Sustained practice leading to improved performance. Refined skills. Development of new skills. Development of concentration and perseverance. Development of the ability to practise independently. Limited decision-making capability through choice of pace of practice or location. Potential for practising at individual level thereby catering to some extent for individual differences.

While the teacher still takes most decisions about what is to be practised and in what way, pupils begin to take some responsibility. They will be able to choose the timing or the pace of the activity. They may also be given choice of location – 'Find a space where you can practise safely' – or of difficulty – 'Begin close to your partner and move further away if you can make five accurate passes easily'.

When to use it?

This is probably the most commonly used style when teaching or working to improve basic skills, for example different passing techniques in games, the service in racket games, simple linked movements in gymnastics (forward roll, stretch jump), a motif in dance. While its key feature is that the teacher is able to go round giving feedback, the use of other strategies in conjunction with this style will affect the relative emphasis given to rote performance, to knowledge or to understanding. For example, the teacher can choose simply to tell the pupils how to improve: 'Begin with a wider stance and transfer your weight as you release the ball': or can ask questions to make the pupil think: 'Which gives you more power, feet together or one foot behind the other? Why?'

It is also appropriate when the teacher wants to retain a strong control over the activity perhaps for safety reasons. This could be when teaching the safe use of the trampette or when introducing a new skill in the gymnasium. It might be needed if the teacher felt that pupils were not ready to take responsibility and were not capable of working independently.

It may also be used where the efficient use of limited time to include maximum activity is a priority.

Examples of tasks

1. Pupils have one bench between three. They are shown how to approach the bench and jump off it as practice for later use of a spring-board. They are then asked to practise concentrating on a double take off from the bench and jumping for height.

2. Pupils have one hockey ball between three. They are asked to decide how far they can hit it and then stand that distance apart and practise accurate drives.

3. Pupils have a volleyball between four. They are asked to practise the volley by trying to keep the ball in the air for as long as possible.

Style	*Characteristics*	*Outcomes*
Style C Reciprocal	Pupils work in pairs. One performs, partner gives feedback. Pupils receive immediate feedback from partner. Teacher communicates through pupil to performer. Emphasis on personal and social skills because of demands on communication skills.	Co-operative behaviour and development of social skills. Development of observational and analytical skills. Development of the ability to evaluate others' performance against given criteria or against self-chosen criteria. Development of communication skills through giving positive and constructive feedback. Practising and refining skills. Understanding and evaluating how well others have achieved. Ability to help others through suggesting approaches to improvement or giving specific technical advice.

The key feature of this style is that pupils work together with one playing the teacher and one the pupil role. Its advantage is that the performer can receive far more feedback than the class teacher can possibly give. In order to help pupils to know what sort of feedback is appropriate, task cards are frequently used with this style. When introducing this style to pupils, it is important to spend time ensuring that all are aware of the qualities needed to play the 'teacher' role effectively, e.g. give praise, be patient, watch carefully. While pupil activity may be reduced pupil learning will not be, since adopting the role of teacher may have a beneficial effect on the pupil's performance when it is his or her turn to be active. For example, in swimming, where pupils often have to work on a paired basis to meet safety requirements, pupils can help each other by looking for particular features of the stroke being practised such as head position in front crawl or the leg action in backstroke.

When to use it?

When personal and social development through pupil interaction is an aim.
To foster evaluation skills.
When increased feedback for pupils is desirable.

Examples of tasks

1. Pupils are asked to work in twos and practise the basketball set shot from a distance chosen by them. Teaching points are written on the blackboard. They take it in turns to practise. Their partner is asked to help them to improve.
2. Pupils, in groups of three, have a worksheet giving several examples of counterbalances to be performed in pairs. A number of teaching points are given on the worksheet. One pupil helps the other two to perform the balances. They change roles so that all have a turn at being both 'teacher' and performer.
3. Pupils work in twos in a swimming lesson, one in the water and one on the side. Teaching points for breast-stroke are written on the white-board. The 'teacher' observes the 'pupil' and gives feedback to improve the stroke.

Style	*Characteristics*	*Outcomes*
Style D Self-check	Pupils assess own learning against given criteria. Shift towards independent learning. Certain level of proficiency needed. Tasks need to be conducive to assessment through reference to 'external' indicators.	Ability to evaluate own performance. Development of sustained independent practice. Adapting and refining skills. Practice and performance.

For this style to be successful, a certain amount of proficiency and understanding is needed so that pupils are able to make a sensible assessment of their success and appreciate how they might improve further. It is more appropriate to some activities than to others. For example it is far more difficult for the performer to assess his or her success or to analyse his or her performance if the activity is fast moving and has little reference to external success criteria. Tumbling skills in the gymnasium are far more difficult to self assess than shots at goal in hockey or basketball, putting the shot or throwing the javelin. For the latter examples the performer can be given clear indicators and guidelines for diagnosing faults. Success in shooting at goal is easily measured as is the distance achieved in a put or throw. Pointers for checking shooting action could be, direction of follow-through, transfer of weight, hand position on stick or ball. For throwing the javelin they could be angle of release and landing, the javelin flight path (smooth or wobbly). In a dance studio use of mirrors can facilitate the use of this style. Video is another means of enabling pupils to assess their own performance.

When to use it?

When pupils are capable of sustained and constructive practice and have developed some skill in evaluating their own performance.

Examples of tasks

1. Pupils are using springboards and trampettes and are jumping for height. A chalk line is drawn on the landing mat and pupils are asked to try to land no further out than the line.
2. Pupils practise dribbling and shooting in hockey. They are asked to aim at targets within the goal and to look particularly at their follow through to improve the accuracy of the shot.

Style	*Characteristics*	*Outcomes*
Style E Inclusion	Allows for individual practice at appropriate difficulty level. Assumes a certain level of self motivation and awareness of limitations if all are to work to their capacity.	Differentiation with potential for learning across wide ability range, provided that pupils make appropriate choices. Ability to evaluate own performance against given criteria and to compare it with that of others. Progression at own pace. Responsibility for own learning in choosing level of performance and pace of progression. Adapting and refining skills and development of new skills. Practice and performance.

This is the first style which plans specifically for individual differences, although they are not excluded from the other styles mentioned so far with the exception of the Command style. The slanted rope is often given as an example of how this style works. A horizontal rope means that all have to clear a uniform height. If the rope is slanted, then each individual can choose the height at which they clear it. Similarly in other activities, a range of options is given to pupils so that they can participate at a level appropriate for them. For example a choice of starting points can be given for shooting practice in basketball or netball. Pupils can be given beams or vaulting apparatus at varying heights and choose that best suited to their size or ability. Guidance may be needed to help pupils to judge the level at which they should be working. Some may need encouragement to challenge themselves further while others may choose a level for which they are not yet ready.

When to use it?

When differentiated opportunities are needed if all are to continue to progress.
Where pupil choice is important.

Examples of tasks

1. Pupils are given a choice of activities, all involving taking their weight on their hands (handstand, handstand from two foot take off, cartwheel, one handed cartwheel). They choose one to practise and move on to a more difficult challenge once they have mastered their original choice.
2. Pupils are given a choice of full size basketballs or smaller balls and a range of starting points. They choose size of ball and distance from the target and practise set shots.

Style	*Characteristics*	*Outcomes*
Style F Guided discovery	Teacher systematically leads pupil to discover a predetermined learning target. Pupil is involved in a process of discovery based upon questioning by teacher. Pupils involved in thinking about answers and learning with understanding. Activities need to	Understanding of work undertaken – tactics, principles of movement, etc.

	be appropriate, i.e. this style is not suitable for activities where experimentation would be unsafe. It will take longer than other styles and so should be used where the ability to work out solutions independently will be important in the future.	

In this style the teacher still determines the goal but guides pupils to learn for themselves through carefully presented tasks or questions or a combination of the two.

For example, pupils might be asked a series of questions to elicit the appropriate response. 'Balance so that you are very stable and can't be pushed over. What sorts of body parts are you using? What level are you at? Now balance so that you can hold still but so that you could easily be pushed over. What sort of body parts are you using? What level are you at? What do you have to do to keep that position? What happens if you move free body parts?' Through asking relevant questions the pupils can be led to appreciate that body tension is needed to hold difficult balances and that the centre of gravity needs to be over the supporting base. They will have discovered that very stable balances involve large body parts or several body parts and are likely to be fairly low level.

In the games context pupils can be asked to try out different body positions when marking and to assess which is the most effective.

When to use it?

When development of understanding is important.
When pupil involvement in the learning process is wanted.

Examples of tasks

1. Pupils are asked to try each of several alternatives and decide which is the most effective. 'At the end of a forward roll, try standing up first with your legs straight, and then with them bent. Which is the easier? Try rolling fast and slowly. Which is the easier to stand up from?'
2. Pupils are asked to try a chest pass first standing with their feet together with no weight transfer and then with feet one behind the other and transferring weight from the back foot as they throw the ball. They are asked which gives the more powerful throw.

Style	*Characteristics*	*Outcomes*
Style G Divergent (or problem-solving)	Teacher presents problem. Pupils are encouraged to find many alternative solutions. There are no finite predetermined answers. An infinite number of solutions could be possible. Appropriate for activities where creativity is important such as gymnastics and dance.	Development of planning and evaluation skills. Development of ability to devise solutions. Compositional skills. Tactical skills.

This style encourages creative thinking in that no one solution is assumed and the outcome cannot necessarily be predicted, although the experienced teacher will have some idea of the kinds of solutions likely to emerge.

When to use it?

Where the development of new ideas is a priority.
Where the ability to think through solutions is important.
Where time is needed for exploration and trying ideas out.

Examples of tasks

1. Pupils are asked to find different ways of starting or ending a forward or backward roll.
2. Pupils are asked to make up a competitive game using a large ball or using lacrosse sticks and balls. (What is the aim of the game? What kinds of pass will be used? What are the limits of the playing area? How do you score? How do you gain possession? How do you start? What do you do if it is not working? What do you do if teams are uneven?)
3. Pupils in a netball team are asked to work out a system for centre passes so that they know who is to receive the ball.

Style	*Characteristics*	*Outcomes*
Style H Individual programme	Teacher decides the general area for study. Learner takes decisions about the detail of what is to be studied. Teacher acts as adviser and facilitator.	Project work such as GCSE. Key Stage 4 work where pupils have options within their chosen activity areas.

Styles H onwards are more likely to be found in higher education or at Key Stage 4 and beyond. The individual programme may be found, for example, in a GCSE practical programme where the teacher decides that gymnastics or dance will be an assessed area and pupils make decisions about the focus of a dance or gymnastics routine. Pupils may choose the focus of the project which constitutes part of the course work for GCSE, GNVQ or A level.

Style	*Characteristics*	*Outcomes*
Style I Learner initiated	Learner takes initiative about content and the learning process. Teacher/supervisor acts in an advisory capacity when approached by the learner.	Independent study such as work for a dissertation or thesis.

This style is more usually identified with independent work in higher education where the student has freedom to suggest topics for a dissertation or thesis and the teacher's role is one of facilitator, responding to questions from the student.

Style	*Characteristics*	*Outcomes*
Style J Self teach	Learner takes full responsibility for the learning process.	Little application in schools at present.

Helping students to develop a range of teaching styles

Most teachers have a preference for one teaching style or group of styles rather than another, and students are no different. Clearly, the more styles the student can draw upon, the greater the flexibility he or she will have when thinking through possible approaches to work with specific classes.

Lack of confidence will tend to result in over reliance on one approach or on a limited range of approaches. The student needs to develop confidence in one approach so that he or she feels there is something to fall back on if attempting a different style causes problems. Obviously the choice of group with whom to try out a new style may be critical. The student should be encouraged to try new approaches with classes with whom he or she feels confident.

Some styles are clearly more demanding in terms of the need for observation or subject knowledge. Students may be helped to use these styles through strategies such as collaborative teaching (see Chapter 9). For example, the use of a problem-solving approach in gymnastics may concern the student who feels that he or she will not be able to see all that is going on and that there may be safety issues. Sharing the lesson with the teacher who takes responsibility for some groups while pupils are working can help resolve the problem and give the student the confidence to persevere with the approach.

Activities for developing understanding of teaching styles

Activity A

Why?

To increase awareness of the relationship between teaching style and learning outcome.

How?

Students should analyse a lesson in terms of the teaching styles used, how successful they were and what the pupils learned. The grid shown as Figure 4.1 may be useful.

Style	Task(s)	Learning outcomes (performance, planning, evaluating, personal, social, health)
A Command		
B Practice		
C Reciprocal		
D Self-check		
E Inclusion		
F Guided discovery		
G Divergent (or problem-solving		
Others		

Figure 4.1

Follow-up discussion

Which teaching styles led to which learning outcomes?

Did some styles facilitate personal/social development outcomes?
Hinder them?
Why?

Did some styles facilitate improved performance?
Hinder it?
Why?

Did some styles facilitate planning and evaluation?
Hinder it?
Why?

Activity B

Why?

To examine how different teachers implement different teaching styles.

How?

Follow the pattern of Activity A, but ask students to observe two different teachers and to complete the same grid (see Figure 4.1).

Follow-up discussion

How did the teachers observed use different teaching styles?

What were similarities/differences?

How do you account for the differences?

Did learning outcomes relate to teaching styles in the same way in both lessons observed?

Were there other factors to explain similarities/differences?

Activity C

Why?

To help student awareness of different teaching styles in practice.

How?

Ask student to identify the teaching styles which he or she anticipates using throughout the lesson. Observe the lesson –

- comparing planned use of styles with actual use
- the extent to which student keeps to the chosen style
- the effectiveness of each learning episode.

Follow-up discussion

How successful did the student feel he or she was in using styles as planned?

What were the reasons for changing from planned use, if this happened?

What did the pupils learn?

Was this what was intended?

What might have been the outcome if a different style had been used?

Were there particular circumstances which affected the success or otherwise of the styles used in this lesson?

Would this work with all groups?

If not, why not?

CHAPTER 5

Teaching Strategies

The previous chapter discussed teaching styles which could be used for episodes within a lesson or throughout a lesson. This chapter looks at more specific strategies, most of which could be employed within the context of several different teaching styles. For each strategy, a number of questions are asked. These could be used as a framework for helping the student to think about a particular strategy, why he or she was using it and how to make it effective. They could help the mentor, when observing the student, to analyse how a strategy is being used, how successful it has been and what might be done to make it more effective. They could also help the mentor to consider how to encourage the student to widen their personal repertoire of strategies – for example, by extending their use of demonstrations to include different purposes or by improving questioning techniques. For more experienced teachers, the questions can form the basis of analysis of their own teaching or for comparing different approaches within a department.

Task setting

What kind of task is being set? Is it about management, that is setting out equipment, organising pupils into groups, organising them into the working space? It is about performance, that is what to do to learn or improve a particular skill or develop a particular strategy or tactic? The following questions may help students to reflect on their own task setting or on that of others whom they observe.

- *Are all pupils listening?* A very common mistake made by beginning teachers is to talk over pupils who are still conducting their own conversations. This is usually the result either of lack of confidence or over-eagerness to get on with the task in hand.
- *Is the language used appropriate? Do all pupils understand?* A useful observation task for a student is to work with a small group of less able pupils and to ask them to interpret what the teacher has just said. By

the time they reach Key Stage 3 some pupils have given up hope of understanding what has been said and rely on watching other pupils and copying. Finding out exactly what pupils do understand can sometimes provide insights into pupils' behaviour. What has been interpreted as misbehaviour and constant off-task behaviour can actually be a result of never understanding the task in the first place.

- *Do pupils know why they are being asked to complete a particular task?* Detailed explanations of 'why' are not needed every time a task is set, but pupils should know what they are expected to know, be able to do and understand by the end of any given unit or work. They then have a context within which the various tasks within a lesson are set.
- *Is the complexity appropriate for the group? Is it too complex? Insufficiently challenging?* A common early mistake is to present pupils with far too much information within a single task and then leave pupils for far too long working on one complex task. With younger pupils or those whose concentration span is limited, several simply explained tasks interspersed with concentrated activity periods are likely to be more effective than one complicated task leading to pupil attention wandering and activity tailing off.
- *Does it allow for different abilities?* Most physical education teaching is to mixed ability groups. Approaches to differentiation were considered in Chapter 3. It is useful to ask in relation to each task, 'What will I expect the most able to do, the least able to do, the average child to do?'
- *Is it presented concisely?* Most analyses of physical education teaching reveal relatively small proportions of active learning time and quite low levels of physical activity over the duration of a lesson. One reason for this is the length of time taken to set tasks and organise pupils. Sometimes the problem is that too much information is being presented. Sometimes the teacher is simply too verbose!
- *Does it sound interesting and motivating?* This is related to confidence and to the effective use of the voice. Lack of confidence can lead to a very dull presentation.

Explaining

Many of the factors identified as important for effective task setting are equally applicable to explaining, especially those related to language use, conciseness and complexity. Other questions might be:

- Could a demonstration replace or supplement the explanation?
- Could pupils be involved in the talking rather than just the teacher?

Observing

The ability to observe and to react to what is seen is absolutely fundamental to good physical education teaching. It becomes even more important where a large class is working on differentiated tasks, where, if the teacher's powers of observation are limited, he or she will not be able to develop the work being produced. Observation is part of the process of formative assessment which occurs in every lesson as teachers provide feedback to pupils on the basis of the observed performance or as a result of answers given to questions. The following procedure is suggested to help students to adopt a safe and effective routine when pupils are working and one which will facilitate the development of observation skills.

- *Is the class working safely?* This will always be a factor although clearly it is a more significant issue in some activity areas (for example, gymnastics, some athletics activities) than others (dance, aerobics). While most pupils tend to avoid attempting tasks beyond their abilities, they may unwittingly be encouraged to do so by peer group pressure or by suggestion by the teacher. Lack of awareness of others may lead to pupils working too close to others for safety or to failing to wait until there is room for them to take their turn safely. Equipment may be positioned so that it becomes unsafe for use, e.g. gymnastics apparatus too close to a wall or window.
- *Is the class answering the task set?* The teacher needs to check this before moving on to anything else. If the task is not being answered, is this because,
  - pupils have not listened
  - there is genuine misunderstanding
  - the task is too difficult or too easy or otherwise inappropriate
  - pupils are deliberately working off-task.
- *How well is the task being answered?*
  - Is a variety of response sought (e.g. in gymnastics or dance)? If so, are the ideas being produced relevant to the task set?
  - Is quality of performance being sought through teaching a specific skill or giving the opportunity to practise a selection of actions?
  - Are all pupils performing with a high rate of success? Is this because the task is too easy?
  - Are most struggling? Can you help or does an easier task need to be set?
- *Which aspects of the work need improvement?*
  - Are there common difficulties which demand some input to the whole class?

– Do one or two individuals need specific help?
– How are you going to phrase the additional input? Remember pupils need to know not only what they need to do, but also how to do it (e.g. rather than say 'Hit the ball further', say 'Step into the shot so that you can hit the ball further').

- *Are there some examples which could be shown to the rest of the class?* Remember to pre-warn pupils that you would like them to demonstrate.
- *Are individuals working to their capacity?* Has the task allowed for this? If not how can the able be extended?

Questioning

The skilful use of questions is an essential part of effective teaching. Questions are used for various purposes and it is important that the teacher is clear about why a particular question is being asked so that it can be phrased accordingly. For example, if the teacher wished to check whether pupils had remembered key points from a previous lesson a question such as, 'Who can tell me what I should do to perform a good lay up shot?' would be a more appropriate form of words than, 'How do you score in basketball.'

Some purposes of questioning are:

- *To make the class think.* Questions in this context are intended to make pupils think about what they are doing rather than simply following instructions with no understanding of the reason for them.

  'Why do you think that I asked you to put the spare netballs back in the bag?'

  'So that nobody could fall over them and hurt themselves.'

- *To keep attention.* As a general principle, if a class expects to be asked questions about a demonstration or explanation then their concentration may well be improved.

  This category relies as much upon how the teacher handles the questioning process as on the form of the question. Pupils need to feel that they may be asked to answer. Teachers therefore ask pupils to put their hands up and wait for a number to do so before asking a child to answer. While it is tempting for the beginning teacher to ask the first child to raise their hand to answer, in gratitude that someone is offering, such a strategy will very quickly lead the rest of the class to sit back secure in the knowledge that they will not be asked for a response. In many contexts several pupils may be asked for their answers, particularly where a number of different answers are acceptable.

For example,

'Why do you think that it might be a good idea to keep your muscles tense when you try to balance?'

'Because it looks better and neater.'

'Yes, what were you going to say John?'

'Because you're less likely to fall over.'

'Yes, what did you think Ramela?'

'You can make your body shape really clear.'

- *To build up or consolidate knowledge.*

  'What shape do your head and hands make when you do a handstand?'

  'What should your finishing position be when you have performed a chest pass?'

  'How many defenders are behind the goal line at a penalty corner?'

- *To provoke thought.*

  'Why do you think James is managing to jump so high?'

  'Can you think of a different finishing position?'

  'How could your team make it more difficult for the others to get into a shooting position?'

- *To test knowledge.*

  'Which players are allowed in the attacking circle?'

  'What happens if there is a double dribble?'

  'What is the difference between canon and unison?'

  'What are the rules about turning in a breast-stroke race?'

- *To revise earlier work.*

  'How many different directions did you practise rolling in last week?'

  'What did you have to remember to perform a good chest pass?'

- *To check knowledge (without probing understanding).*

  'What do we call the part of the body which pumps blood?'

  'What is the name of this pass?'

- *To test understanding.*

  'Why does your heart rate go up when you have been running round the gym more than when you have done some press ups?'

- *To emphasise particular teaching points.*

  'Where does Winston place his feet to make it easy to stand up at the end of the roll?'

  'Where is Jane's stick pointing at the end of her follow-through?'

  'Where was Hayley positioned in order to intercept that pass?'

- *To help the pupils' observation and thereby increase understanding.*

  'Watch Judith. How does she use her arms to help her to keep her balance?'

  'Look at Sukh's set shot. What do you notice about the position of his hands and fingers?'

- *To motivate and stimulate.*

  'Can you jump any higher?'

  'Can you swim more widths than last time?'

- *To obtain feedback.* Questions under this heading can be used to determine ability, understanding, recall, skill level and so on.

  'Why were some balances easier to hold than others?'

  'What factors will affect how far you throw the javelin?'

  'How many of you feel confident about taking your weight on your hands without a supporter?'

- *To develop reflection and assessment.*

  'Why do you think that Carol's performance was good?'

  'How did Carl get variety into his sequence?'

'What helped the reds to get into a goal-scoring position?'

- *To give many pupils the opportunity to show knowledge or understanding*. The target of the question rather than its form is important here. Answering questions can be an important form of achievement for pupils who find physical performance difficult.

In addition to serving different purposes, questions can demand different kinds of responses from pupils. Questions which test knowledge are sometimes referred to as lower order questions while those which create knowledge are known as higher order questions (Brown and Wragg, 1993).

There will be many occasions when the first question does not elicit the desired answer. Indeed it may not elicit any answer at all! The temptation to provide the answer and move quickly on should be resisted. Students will often need help in rephrasing questions in this situation. The following strategies may help:

- Do not be afraid to wait for an answer! This is especially important if the question is complex. A common fault among inexperienced teachers is to panic and answer the question for the class who very soon learn that there is no need for them to make any effort because if they wait the teacher will answer for them.
- Word questions so that they are clear, precise and relevant to the age and ability of the class. A vague question such as 'What about your arms?' gives pupils little chance of understanding what you mean or of constructing a reasonable answer.
- If no one offers an answer rephrase the question *or* simplify it (see below for how to do this). It may be that pupils are not sure about your own line of thinking or it may be that they simply do not understand.
- Order questions in a logical and meaningful way. Make the follow up question more specific.
- Give prompts to help pupils.
- Encourage hesitant pupils. Ask the question before naming a pupil who is to answer. If the pupil is named first, the rest of the class have no need to think of the answer.
- Ask a probing question to elicit further information.
- Ask an 'either/or' question.
- Ask an elliptical question (that is one where the pupil supplies a missing word).

Students may need help to avoid common mistakes such as:

- lack of clarity (volume/speed of speech);
- language which is not understood;

- questions which are too complex;
- too many closed questions;
- poor targetting (e.g. only accessible to the most able);
- irrelevant to lesson episode;
- taking answers from one or very few pupils;
- ignoring answers;
- rejecting answers which are correct but not what was expected.

Demonstrations

Demonstrations can be used to serve several different purposes.

- *To show a technical point.* This could be how to position the head and hands in a headstand, the hand and finger position in a set shot, the starting position for a shot putt, the arm action in breast-stroke and so on. It is important that what is demonstrated will actually prove helpful. For example, if what is required is a demonstration of the placing of the hands and the initial arm movement for a handspring, then this should be shown rather than a spectacular performance of the whole skill (although there is of course a place for showing the whole action). A demonstration of something which appears to be well beyond pupils' capability can be intimidating rather than motivating if given at an inappropriate time. It may also distract from the real focus of the demonstration. For example, a set shot demonstrated at a great distance from the basket may lead to attention focusing on the distance from which the shot has been made rather than on the technical points which are being stressed.
- *To show something well done.* Where the teacher is working to improve quality of performance, e.g. in gymnastics or dance or technical skill, e.g. in swimming, a demonstration of the this type may be used to illustrate the standard expected or the next stage of progression. For quality of performance, the level of skill is not relevant but the way in which it is performed is vital. It can therefore be a good opportunity to choose a pupil whose ability in terms of technical skill is low, but who can show good poise and finish.
- *To show a range of possibilities.* This kind of demonstration can be useful when exploratory work has been carried out and can very easily involve a number of pupils of varying abilities. Alternatively half the class could show their ideas while the other half watch to see how many ideas they can identify.
- *To compare different aspects of work.* In swimming two pupils could be asked to demonstrate front crawl, one breathing to the right and one breathing bilaterally. This could be used to compare the advantages and disadvantages of the two methods.

- *To explain a particular concept and establish its features.* This might be used to explain the concepts of symmetry and asymmetry in gymnastics or to show what is meant by a zoned defence, where the emphasis is less on how to do something and more on establishing exactly what it means.
- *To emphasise particular teaching points.* This sort of demonstration may be in response to a whole class finding a particular aspect of an activity difficult, whether this be a technical point such as follow-through in a throwing action or improving quality such as maintaining body tension to sustain a balance.
- *To stimulate more ambitious movement.* This is particularly relevant in situations where pupils have a choice of response. It may be that one or two pupils have tried a particular answer but that the majority are producing answers which, while not inappropriate, are not challenging them. The teacher might ask a pupil to show for example a forward roll to straddle finish and suggest that this is well within the capability of many other pupils.
- *To show a fault or faults.* As a general rule, the teacher should demonstrate if faults are being shown rather than embarrass pupils in front of their peers.
- *To show completed work.* In gymnastics or dance where composition and performance are integral to the activity, performance of completed dances or gymnastics sequences should be a feature of lessons. This sort of demonstration also provides very good opportunities for encouraging pupils to evaluate the work of others and for the teacher to make a judgement about pupil performance.
- *To show something original or otherwise outstanding.* Situations sometimes arise in PE where a pupil who is particularly gifted and involved in out of school training is performing at a level well beyond that of his or her peers. A judgement has to be made by the teacher about the advisability of showing aspects of this work to the rest of the class. Sometimes pupils become very arrogant about their performance and the teacher would feel that any encouragement to 'show off' should be avoided. Others are very modest about their achievements and would be very reluctant to demonstrate in front of their peers. For others, their achievements may be a real source of self-esteem which will enhanced by an opportunity to perform in front of their classmates.

Organising demonstrations

- *Who should demonstrate?* The teacher? One pupil to the whole class? One pupil to the rest of their group? A group of pupils? Half the class?

Decisions will depend upon the purpose of the demonstration.

- *Can everyone see?* It may be necessary to ask observers to move either so that their view is not obstructed or so that they have a particular view of what is being shown. For example, pupils need to see a headspring from the side in order to see the angle of the legs and the position of the hips. They need to be at the side to see the follow-through in a throw or a hockey pass. More generally observers should be positioned for minimal distraction. This means, for example, not looking into the sun, with other activities going on behind observers rather than in front of them.
- *Do the pupils involved know what they are supposed to be doing?* Have they been informed in advance that they are going to be asked – there is nothing more disconcerting for a beginning teacher than to be met with outright refusal, having asked someone to demonstrate unexpectedly. Little better is finding that the pupil has completely forgotten what it is he or she was doing a few moments earlier, resulting in a totally unexpected and inappropriate demonstration. This is especially important where a pupil has produced several answers to a task.
- *What are the observers to look for?* Apart from the importance of pointing out key features, if that is the purpose of the demonstration, it is an opportunity for observation, analysis and evaluation by pupils which should not be missed. Initially, pupils need specific guidelines:

  'Look at these two headstands and notice particularly the triangle made by the position of head and hands.'

  'Watch the other half and choose two which you think have linked their actions together particularly smoothly.'

  'Watch these two passing the ball and tell me why you think that Judith is always able to catch the ball easily.'

Later pupils may be encouraged to suggest observation criteria for themselves.

CHAPTER 6
Assessing Pupils

It is important that students understand certain key concepts related to assessment so that they can implement assessment policies with understanding and confidence and in ways which are equitable for all pupils.

What do we mean by assessment?

Put simply, assessment involves making judgements about pupils for specific purposes. Different approaches to assessment reflect different philosophies and will have different effects upon those involved in their use. Within physical education, teachers use a variety of approaches during their day to day work.

Approaches to Assessment

Ipsative assessment

This means that performance is compared with one's own previous best and is assessed irrespective of what others have achieved. It indicates whether a pupil has improved or not and how much progress has been made. For example, Pat swam 20 metres last term and this term he swam 50 metres. Judith ran 9 laps in a 12 minute run last year and this year she ran 11 laps. Using this approach it would be possible for everyone in a class to achieve a high grade because all had improved on an earlier performance, even if the level of the better performance was very low.

Ipsative assessment will record progression but not necessarily absolute performance levels. It should motivate those whose achievement will never match that of their peers.

Norm-referenced assessment

This means assessing a pupil's performance in relation to standards achieved within a given group. It enables comparison of one pupil against another. For example, the average distance swum by Pat's year group is 75 metres. Pat can swim 50 metres. His performance will be recorded as below average or relatively weak. The average distance run by Judith's class is 12 laps. Judith's performance is described as slightly below average. By definition, some members of any group will record a poor performance. Selection of representative teams involves making norm-referenced judgements, since choosing the best players involves making comparisons with the cohort available rather than against absolute standards. An U13 team could well be able to beat an U14 team because average standards of play are higher in Year 8 than in Year 9.

Norm-referenced assessment will record performance level but not progression. It will motivate the successful but may well have the opposite effect on others.

Criterion-referenced assessment

This means assessing an individual's performance against previously set criteria. It assesses the extent to which agreed goals have been achieved. For example, the criterion might be that pupils should be able to swim 25 metres by the age of 11. Pat, by swimming 50 metres, more than meets this requirement. The criterion for the 12 minute run might be set at 10 laps. Judith therefore meets this standard.

There are no predetermined limits on the number of pupils who can achieve the expected standard. Governing body awards use criterion-referenced assessment in that all pupils who can demonstrate the requisite skills may gain the award. It should motivate pupils by giving them clear goals for which to aim, provided that these are realistic and can provide a summative judgement about performance.

Formative assessment

Formative assessment takes place during the learning process. Its purpose is to describe progress and to identify pupils' needs. It may utilise a whole range of assessment strategies in order to inform teaching decisions on a day to day basis. Formative assessment is likely to be that used primarily by students and teachers in meeting the DFE requirement to use 'assessment in their teaching', although HMI evidence suggests that it is not used as effectively or as widely as it might be.

> Many pupils were not being given a sufficiently clear idea of their progress or an indication of how they might improve the quality of their work (DES, 1992).

Martin is playing a 4 v 4 game of basketball. He positions himself well to receive the ball and his catching and passing skills are good, with the result that he is very involved in the game. Whenever he gets the ball within range of the basket he shoots with little success although from close in he can score. Which of these two examples of feedback would be more effective in the context of formative assessment?

'Martin, your shooting is way off target. Pass the ball to someone else whose aim is better.'

'Martin, your passing and catching are excellent. If you were to move under the basket to catch the ball you would have a much better chance of scoring.'

Summative assessment

This takes place at the end of a unit of work and aims to measure and record attainment through summarising pupil achievement rather than to influence teaching. The information may be provided for pupils, for parents, for governors, for employers, for other teachers or for any combination of these. Harlen (1991) describes two approaches to summative assessment as summing up and checking up. The former is essentially a summary of the formative assessments which will have been made over a period of time while the latter collects 'new' information about a pupil, usually through some form of test.

Recording achievement is one way of summarising aspects of formative assessment in that it gives the pupil the opportunity to describe their current level of achievement over a range of indicators and to set themselves targets for the immediate future.

If summative assessment is based only on the formative assessments made, then the outcome depends upon the pupil having had the opportunity to show skill, knowledge or understanding. It may also be based upon information which is now out of date. This can be particularly true of physical education where pupils may well be involved in activities out of school and be given opportunities to extend their learning and their performance independently of the school.

Amanda's swimming record shows that she can just swim a width of backcrawl following three weeks of concentration on this stroke and that her best stroke is breast-stroke in which she can swim 50 metres comfortably with reasonably good technique. However by the end of the Year Amanda can actually swim more efficiently on her back than on her front, having been practising at the local pool at weekends.

'Checking up' in the form of tests does give all pupils a chance to show what they have learned. On the other hand they take a long time and decisions have to be taken as to whether the loss of teaching time can be justified for the additional information provided.

Why assess?

- to help pupils improve
- to help pupils to diagnose their strengths and weaknesses
- to help pupils to work at a level appropriate for them
- to provide pupils with feedback on their performance
- to record pupil achievement

- to provide teachers with feedback on teaching programmes
- to help teachers to meet learning objectives and to plan for this
- to help teachers to identify individual pupil needs
- to enable teacher to record pupil achievement

- to provide information for interested parties – parents, governors, other teachers
- to help parents to understand their child's development and progress
- to provide employers with relevant information about a pupil's skills, qualities and experiences
- to provide governors with evidence of departmental and pupil achievement

- to select for limited opportunities, e.g. places in a team
- to discriminate between individuals, e.g. those suitable for A level study and those who are not.

Some of the above apply to assessment at all stages of the pupil's school career. Others would be particularly relevant at specific stages, e.g. at the end of units of work, at transfer from one school to another, when leaving school.

What does assessment involve?

Teachers and students need to:

- *Know what they want pupils to learn.* This may appear to be stating the obvious, but, for the beginning teacher, clarifying exactly what the focus for a lesson is can be an important part of the planning process. For example, asking pupils to work in groups of three or four to plan a gymnastics sequence could have a number of outcomes:
  - pupils could demonstrate high levels of individual skill with few common elements to the work

- pupils could assist each other, e.g. by including partner balances or supported activities
- pupils could plan a piece of work in which each individual included two movements of his or her choice but which also included some common actions
- one pupil could 'choreograph' the work of all the others.

The judgements which the teacher made about the work would depend upon whether his or her learning priorities were:

- individual performance in which the first outcome would be acceptable
- effective group interaction in which the second outcome would be acceptable
- appreciation of the strengths and limitations of group members in which case the third outcome would be acceptable
- group roles including leadership in which case the fourth outcome would be acceptable.

If the teacher is not clear about the possible outcomes from a particular learning activity then he or she will find it difficult to make an assessment of what has been learned. If the teacher's anticipated outcome is not achieved it is easy to jump to the conclusion that the pupils have not learned anything when, in fact, they have learned something equally worthwhile.

- *Recognise what is and what is not assessable.* This is particularly important at a time when physical education, in common with other subjects, is expected to be accountable. Teachers therefore need to be able to demonstrate to senior staff, to parents and to governors that their programmes have clearly articulated aims and that they achieve these. For example, the aim of preparing pupils to lead active adult lives is very laudable and few would disagree with its inclusion. Its achievement is not however assessable in the short term. Other objectives are therefore needed against which the programme may be judged.
- *Have analysed the development and progression involved in the learning process.* Without understanding of the various learning stages involved in specific activities, the teacher will find it difficult to judge whether or not a pupil is making progress towards achieving success or whether he or she needs guidance to change aspects of technique or strategy. For example, moving from successful performance of a skill unopposed to its successful performance in the game situation is an example of progression. If a pupil cannot perform a skill under pressure in a game, the solution will not be to return to practising the skill unopposed but to try with passive or half speed opposition, thereby providing a stepping stone to its performance in the full game situation.
- *Provide opportunities for pupils to learn.* If pupils are to learn new

skills and tactics they need time to practise and refine their actions. This means that they need to learn to practise effectively without constant intervention by the teacher.

- *Identify sources of evidence of attainment/achievement*. Teacher observation will provide a lot of evidence of performance but not necessarily of understanding or knowledge. Other sources of evidence are important, particularly for pupils who find performance difficult but may nevertheless have a very good understanding of principles of play or the factors involved in the successful performance of a gymnastics skill. Assessment of the planning and evaluation component of the physical education attainment target requires more than simply observing pupils perform. Some other sources of evidence might be:

  – pupil self assessments or peer assessments
  – written materials, e.g. notes, diaries, workbooks, written descriptions or plans, diagrams of patterns of play, sequences
  – group discussions
  – answers to questions
  – pupil explanations or descriptions.

The teacher needs to be able to provide constructive feedback to pupils at all times, and to make an assessment of attainment or progress from time to time. Evidence of achievement is often easy to see, for example the pupil succeeds in swimming a width non-stop, or in standing up at the end of a forward roll without using hands, or succeeds in scoring from a set shot. At other times it is less obvious, for example the pupil has developed a reasonably effective arm and leg swimming action but head position is tilting the body so far from horizontal that he or she is unable to swim more than a few strokes. In the gymnasium, the pupil is tucking up and placing his or her feet close to the hips during the forward roll but is leaving the shoulders behind so that all momentum is lost. The action of the hands in the set shot is correct but the body is tipping slightly sideways so that the ball goes to the side of the basket. In these cases the teacher needs to identify what has been achieved and what needs further work.

Principles of effective assessment

- assessment should be on the basis of agreed criteria which are known to pupils
- criteria used should reflect expected educational development and progression
- formative assessment should not interfere with normal teaching and learning
- assessment should be related to a manageable recording and reporting system.

Developing assessment criteria

1. Establish general assessment criteria related to each EKSD.
2. Establish activity-specific criteria related to the general criteria: that is, what do you want the pupils to learn within the activity area, and in what order?
3. Relate activity specific assessment criteria/learning outcomes to the units of work within your programme.
4. Make decisions about assessment, recording and reporting strategies.

Remember that the end result needs to be manageable! There is no requirement to assess everything at the end of every block of work.

Examples

Example 1

This is an example of a recording sheet for a unit of work at Key Stage 3 (see Figure 6.1). It is designed to be used in conjunction with the class register, thereby avoiding a separate and additional task for the teacher.

Example 2

This is an example of a simple form for recording progress and achievement during a key stage (see Figure 6.2, adapted from Spackman, 1995).

Example 3

Good practice often involves pupils in the assessment process. This not only provides further evidence for the teacher by providing indicators of how pupils see themselves but can also be a valuable starting point for the teacher's thinking about individual pupils. Both Carroll (1994) and Mawer (1995) provide examples of pupils self assessment forms. Another example is shown as Figure 6.3.

Recording pupils' achievement

Related to assessment is the development of Records of Achievement (ROAs) which give pupils opportunities to make teachers aware of any relevant achievement in addition to what has been achieved within physical education lessons. The increasing availability of sophisticated IT equipment in schools, including desk top publishing (DTP) packages,

<table>
<tr><td>KS3, YR8</td><td colspan="4">Assessment aim A</td><td colspan="3">Assessment aim B</td><td colspan="4">Assessment aim C</td></tr>
<tr><td>Invasion games</td><td colspan="4">Develop strategies</td><td colspan="3">Extend skills</td><td colspan="4">Apply strategies</td></tr>
<tr><td>Key
1. Working towards
2. Can do
3. Can do well</td><td colspan="4">Assessment criteria
Beating a defender in an overload situation (4 v 2)</td><td colspan="3">Assessment criteria
Control the ball with consistency and under pressure</td><td colspan="4">Assessment criteria
Recognise and play attacking and defensive role</td></tr>
<tr><td></td><td></td><td colspan="3">A</td><td colspan="3">B</td><td colspan="3">C</td><td></td></tr>
<tr><td>NAME</td><td>Attendance</td><td>1</td><td>2</td><td>3</td><td>1</td><td>2</td><td>3</td><td>1</td><td>2</td><td>3</td><td>Kit</td></tr>
<tr><td>Andrews Mark</td><td></td><td></td><td></td><td></td><td></td><td></td><td></td><td></td><td></td><td></td><td></td></tr>
<tr><td>Anthony Clare</td><td></td><td></td><td></td><td></td><td></td><td></td><td></td><td></td><td></td><td></td><td></td></tr>
<tr><td>Bloom Adrienne</td><td></td><td></td><td></td><td></td><td></td><td></td><td></td><td></td><td></td><td></td><td></td></tr>
<tr><td>Boxer Mandy</td><td></td><td></td><td></td><td></td><td></td><td></td><td></td><td></td><td></td><td></td><td></td></tr>
<tr><td>Brixton John</td><td></td><td></td><td></td><td></td><td></td><td></td><td></td><td></td><td></td><td></td><td></td></tr>
<tr><td>Bromfield Solomon</td><td></td><td></td><td></td><td></td><td></td><td></td><td></td><td></td><td></td><td></td><td></td></tr>
<tr><td>Christie Sally</td><td></td><td></td><td></td><td></td><td></td><td></td><td></td><td></td><td></td><td></td><td></td></tr>
<tr><td>Clover Nathan</td><td></td><td></td><td></td><td></td><td></td><td></td><td></td><td></td><td></td><td></td><td></td></tr>
<tr><td>Drew Neil</td><td></td><td></td><td></td><td></td><td></td><td></td><td></td><td></td><td></td><td></td><td></td></tr>
<tr><td>Durbin Geoffrey</td><td></td><td></td><td></td><td></td><td></td><td></td><td></td><td></td><td></td><td></td><td></td></tr>
<tr><td>Eccles Kelly</td><td></td><td></td><td></td><td></td><td></td><td></td><td></td><td></td><td></td><td></td><td></td></tr>
<tr><td>Exbury Tim</td><td></td><td></td><td></td><td></td><td></td><td></td><td></td><td></td><td></td><td></td><td></td></tr>
<tr><td>Glover Matthew</td><td></td><td></td><td></td><td></td><td></td><td></td><td></td><td></td><td></td><td></td><td></td></tr>
<tr><td>Harvey Winston</td><td></td><td></td><td></td><td></td><td></td><td></td><td></td><td></td><td></td><td></td><td></td></tr>
<tr><td>Jones Evan</td><td></td><td></td><td></td><td></td><td></td><td></td><td></td><td></td><td></td><td></td><td></td></tr>
<tr><td>Kaur Ravinder</td><td></td><td></td><td></td><td></td><td></td><td></td><td></td><td></td><td></td><td></td><td></td></tr>
<tr><td>Khan Naseem</td><td></td><td></td><td></td><td></td><td></td><td></td><td></td><td></td><td></td><td></td><td></td></tr>
<tr><td>Matthews Jane</td><td></td><td></td><td></td><td></td><td></td><td></td><td></td><td></td><td></td><td></td><td></td></tr>
<tr><td>Singh Sukbir</td><td></td><td></td><td></td><td></td><td></td><td></td><td></td><td></td><td></td><td></td><td></td></tr>
<tr><td>Thomas Jenny</td><td></td><td></td><td></td><td></td><td></td><td></td><td></td><td></td><td></td><td></td><td></td></tr>
<tr><td>Troughton Hugh</td><td></td><td></td><td></td><td></td><td></td><td></td><td></td><td></td><td></td><td></td><td></td></tr>
<tr><td>Wall Jack</td><td></td><td></td><td></td><td></td><td></td><td></td><td></td><td></td><td></td><td></td><td></td></tr>
<tr><td>Williams Emily</td><td></td><td></td><td></td><td></td><td></td><td></td><td></td><td></td><td></td><td></td><td></td></tr>
<tr><td>Wolley Jo</td><td></td><td></td><td></td><td></td><td></td><td></td><td></td><td></td><td></td><td></td><td></td></tr>
</table>

Figure 6.1

Record of Progress and Attainment – Physical Education	
Name:	Key Stage:
Unit of work	Evidence
Gymnastics – planning and composition; refining and increasing range of actions; cope with success and limitations	
Games (winter) – devising strategies and tactics; development of variety of techniques; appreciate strengths and limitations	
Games (summer) – devising strategies and tactics; development of variety of techniques; appreciate strengths and limitations	
Dance – composition, performance with control and sensitivity to style	
Swimming – two recognised strokes; apply rescue and resuscitation techniques	
HRE – preparation and recovery from exercise; effects of exercise on body systems; role of exercise in maintenance of health	

Figure 6.2

Performance task

Plan and perform a sequence which uses all the apparatus to include:

- one group balance involving everyone
- the involvement of everyone in one partner balance
- each member of the group using all pieces of apparatus
- variety and contrast

Assessment task

Decide on the criteria you are going to use to judge the performance (no more than 4) and write them on the back of this sheet in the left hand column

Look at each of the criteria you have chosen and decide what will be the difference between a very good, an acceptable and a poor performance

Watch the sequence at least twice

Write your judgements and your reasons in the right hand column

Criteria (4 at most)	Judgements and comments

Figure 6.3 Pupil involvement in assessing and recording in gymnastics

means that provision of booklets for this purpose is now within the capability of all physical education departments, maybe with a little assistance from others with information technology expertise. Because ROAs are essentially a record for the pupil, they can include much information which, while very relevant to a number of situations, would not be appropriate as formally assessed elements, particularly in the context of National Curriculum assessment requirements which are closely tied to the given Programme of Study and EKSDs.

Recording and reporting

Schools will have their own systems for the formal recording of progress and reporting to parents. What is equally if not more important is the day to day informal reporting to pupils on their progress. This is particularly true of a subject like physical education where the outcome of the pupils' efforts are immediately visible and public.

'Well done Sarah, that's the best pass I've seen you make and it led to a really good goal.'

'Your sequence work has really improved Mark. If you concentrate on firm muscles and straight legs all the way through and practise your headstand to keep your balance, it will look even better.'

'I'm disappointed in your work today Anne. You can play very well when you make the effort but you need to concentrate on practising as well as wanting to play the game.'

Assessment activities

Activity A

Assessing pupils as an observation task

Discuss with the student the learning outcomes of the lesson and encourage him or her to identify indicators which would provide information about whether pupils were achieving them. For example, if a learning outcome was the use of a specified skill such as a chest pass in a game situation, assessment indicators might be observation of whether the pass was (a) used at all, (b) used when unopposed or used when under pressure, and (c) used at the right time, i.e. over a short rather than a long distance and when the marking enabled the pass to be made successfully. If a learning outcome was intelligent use of stretching exercises to warm up, the task might be to work in pairs and take turns to select an exercise and assessment indicators might be (a) choice of exercises which stretched different muscles in turn, (b) stretching statically without bouncing, and (c) holding the stretch for an appropriate time. If a learning outcome was understanding of the principles of maintaining 'difficult' balances, the student would be expected to appreciate that, while observation might give some indication, it would not be sufficient and other indicators would be needed such as asking questions of the pupils.

Activity B

Assessing pupils in the context of lesson planning

Where students have been given responsibility for the teaching of a unit of work, assessment of pupils' response to the lessons should form the basis of subsequent planning. If assessment indicators are built into the plan, then evaluation of the lesson in relation to these will enable the student to make sensible decisions about the content of the next lesson. (See Chapter 2 for more information about including assessment criteria in lesson plans.) For example, a dance lesson might include the teaching of a short motif followed by a single variation. Pupils are then asked to work in twos or threes to develop a further variation on the motif, showing different relationships. The evaluation of the lesson includes the following:

> All the pupils succeeded in performing the motif accurately as far as the actual movements were concerned but only Hayley and Mark really showed any quality. The rest had little poise or real style. They worked very well in twos and threes – giving them the choice was a good idea but their ideas were very limited. Most worked standing one behind the other and simply repeated the motif in canon. I suppose this is because we were working on following and canon a few weeks ago. Next time I must help them with ideas such as facing each other, back to back, side by side and also the possibilities of unison or one starting very shortly after the other.

There is clear evidence here of the assessment of pupil performance and scrutiny of the plan for the next lesson will reveal the extent to which the student has been successful in planning to develop the areas of weakness identified.

Activity C

Assessing pupils' practical performance and moderating

Video a GCSE group playing in a game situation. Provide students with the assessment criteria for the achievement of different GCSE marks or gradings and ask them to assess selected pupils and to justify their grading. Do the same and use as the basis for discussion about achieving consistency in gradings.

What grade has been given?
For what reason? What was the evidence?
What would have been needed to award a higher grade?
Explain the difference in the grades given to different pupils.

Activity D

Arrange for students to attend a moderation meeting, either departmental or, if possible, inter-school for GCSE. Observing the process of discussing borderline gradings and reaching decisions is a valuable learning opportunity and will help student understanding of factors such as standards to be expected of pupils at a particular age or stage.

Activity E

Give student a reasonably representative set of GCSE assignments which have already been marked by an experienced teacher and ask him or her to mark them. Use as basis for a discussion at a weekly meeting, to compare notes – go through some examples in detail, discussing why a particular mark was given and what would raise it or lower it.

Activity F

Ask two students to write progress reports on the same identified pupils according to the school's reporting policy. If there is only one student in the department ask him or her to write reports on student whom you will be reporting on. Compare the results. Ask the following questions:

Does the report tell you what the pupil can do at present?
Does the report give indicators for future progress?
Will the report be comprehensible by a lay person?
Is the language constructive?

CHAPTER 7

Entitlement to Learning for All – Equal Opportunity Issues

Equal opportunity issues apply to all pupils, boys and girls, pupils from different cultural groups and pupils with special educational needs, the latter including pupils who find learning in physical education problematic and those who are exceptionally gifted. Of course they also apply to student teachers who have an entitlement to equitable treatment when placed in a school.

The working group set up to advise on the statutory framework for the physical education national curriculum made a number of important points about equality of opportunity.

> As a leading and guiding principle for physical education, equal opportunity requires that teachers should treat all children as individuals with their own abilities, difficulties and attitudes (DES, 1991, p16).

The working group goes on to identify a number of issues specific to physical education which need to be considered by teachers who are looking at how best to address equal opportunity considerations. These are:

(a) the public nature of success and failure in physical education;
(b) the competitive nature of many physical education activities;
(c) the legacy of single sex teaching and teacher education in physical education;
(d) moves towards mixed sex grouping, sometimes without an education rationale, and without consideration of the conditions under which mixed sex teaching and single sex teaching might be more successful or appropriate;
(e) the biological and cultural effects of being male or female on the behaviours considered appropriate for girls and boys of different cultures;
(f) the physical nature of physical education, and the emergence of sexuality during key stages 2, 3 and 4, providing both problems and opportunities for physical education in challenging body images, sex stereotypes and other limited perspectives which constrain the choices and achievements of disabled children, and of both girls and boys;
(g) the effects of some culturally restricted interpretations of masculinity on the place and value of dance in the school curriculum, and on boys' opportunities for dance experience and education;
(h) the barriers to young people's involvement caused by the restrictive ways

some sports and forms of dance are portrayed and practised;
(i) the rich potential for physical education to transcend categories of race, sex and learning need, through nurturing the value of individual contributions in group situations, and through presenting a wide range of cultural forms and experiences which reflect our multi-cultural society; and
(j) the treatment of physical education in the sex discrimination legislation and the varied levels of understanding of its effect on curriculum physical education, extra-curricular activities and school sport. (DES, 1991, p17)

These points make a useful framework for consideration of issues which both students and more experienced teachers need to think about.

Issues

What do we mean by equal opportunity?

Equal access to the same curriculum?
Equal success levels in physical education?
A different but equivalent curriculum?
The same curriculum but taught to single sex groups?
Equal participation levels outside and post school?
Access to a relevant curriculum for all? Who decides what is relevant?

It goes without saying that equality of access in physical education will not result automatically in equality of outcome or practice. For example when boys and girls are both taught dance, where previously it appeared only on the girls' physical education curriculum, there is evidence from both teachers and pupils that boys' responses can be negative, affecting both behaviour and learning. Learning and achievement are far from equal. Other activities, for example soccer, may well have considerable appeal for some female pupils, but only if taught in a way which enables them to learn and succeed. Thus single sex teaching may well provide learning opportunities for both sexes where mixed sex groupings are not successful because of the differences in previous experience.

Access to the same curriculum may simply not be a realistic opportunity for some pupils with special educational needs. Grass playing areas may not be accessible to a pupil in a wheelchair. Some gymnastics activities using high apparatus may not be accessible to a pupil with epilepsy. Those making the school policy have to consider what is genuinely inaccessible and what is, in reality, inconvenient rather than inaccessible.

As far as extra-curricular opportunity is concerned, it is easy to claim equal access when in practice various factors ensure that access remains far from equal. Where an activity has traditionally been dominated by one group, whether this be pupils from one sex or from a particular cultural group, others can easily be discouraged from joining. Indeed the dominant group may well ensure that they remain dominant by making sure that others know that they will not be welcome.

Current OFSTED evidence (OHMCI, 1995) suggests that boys have more opportunity to be involved in extra-curricular activity than girls. Is this lack of interest on the part of female pupils or lack of availability of staff? Are the extra-curricular activities that are offered to girls of limited appeal? There is some evidence that extra-curricular provision is largely team games whereas female activity preferences are for individual sports or for non-competitive activities (Williams and Woodhouse, 1996). It has been suggested in the past that involvement in extra-curricular activity is problematic for some ethnic minority pupils, particularly Muslim boys and girls, and that this reflects a lack of interest generally. A recent study fails to find any evidence to support lack of interest in the physical education curriculum and suggests that there is also support for extra-curricular programmes from many of these pupils provided that they are timetabled to take account of their other commitments.

Access to the curriculum means more than being physically present. Pupils may be present at a lesson but have restricted access to learning. The child who is given a whistle and asked to referee each week is not being offered learning opportunities consistent with the requirements of the National Curriculum.

How does an equal opportunities policy impact upon curriculum content?

To what extent does the physical education curriculum cater for diverse groups with diverse interests and requirements? Has the move towards mixed sex physical education, to single departments (led disproportionately by male heads of department) and to single school policies, rather than separate ones for boys and girls, increased or reduced curriculum breadth?

There is considerable evidence that team games, and, in particular invasion games, continue to dominate the physical education curriculum and this is to be actively encouraged by the most recent government initiative, articulated in *Sport: Raising the Game* (Department of National Heritage, 1995). There is equally plentiful evidence that female activity preferences are for individual sports and for non-competitive activity. Is a curriculum which offers all pupils content which is significantly more interesting and relevant to one sex than to another providing equality of opportunity?

Is physical education clothing appropriate for mixed sex work?

In all activities, but especially in dance and gymnastics, where presentation and performance are key elements of the activities, it is important that pupils feel comfortable and at ease with their appearance. Embarrassment and self-consciousness can only have an adverse effect on both learning and performance.

I do not think that we should be made to do things in front of boys when we are only wearing gym knickers and T-shirts (*13 year old girl*).

Our religion does not allow us to show our legs and bodies in public but our teachers try to make us (*15 year old girl*).

The girls are allowed to wear tracksuits but we have to wear our shorts – it's not fair (*13 year old boy*).

Where cultural factors require that the body should be covered in the presence of unrelated males, lack of sensitivity may result in pupils absenting themselves from physical education altogether.

It is easy to underestimate the negative effect that the wearing of inappropriate clothing can have on adolescent pupils. It is also all too easy to find examples of pupils being expected to wear clothing which contradicts all that they have been taught about safe exercise and the importance of warm muscles. Pupils should be able to wear tracksuits, sweaters/sweatshirts, leggings or tights or other appropriate clothing to keep them warm and to reinforce the message given to them elsewhere about warming up and keeping warm during exercise.

Are mixed sex groupings the best way of providing equal opportunities? Always? In some contexts? For some activities? In some schools? For some teachers?

> Choices of mixed or single sex groupings in physical education should be made for educational reasons and after considering the conditions under which they might be most successful and appropriate (DES, 1991, p57).

Unfortunately mixed sex groupings can also be introduced for economic reasons and because of lack of resources. The legacy of single sex teaching and, equally significant, single sex teacher education cannot be ignored when making decisions.

There have been some far from successful attempts to introduce mixed sex soccer at the beginning of Key Stage 3 where boys' greater previous experience combine with attitudinal factors to ensure that the girls' experience is a negative one in spite of considerable interest in the game among the girls. Equally, dance has been taught to mixed sex groups with the reverse effect exacerbated by the fact that the boys' dislike of the activity eventually affected the girls' learning opportunities adversely.

If mixed sex teaching is to be successful several factors including uniform, discussed above, have to be considered.

- Do boys and girls receive equal attention in mixed sex groups? Should they? When? Why?
- Are male and female pupils chosen equally to demonstrate? What are the implications of always choosing pupils from one sex?
- Will any cultural issues affect the success or otherwise of mixed sex work?

This is a question for each individual school to address. While respect for different cultures should be a cornerstone of every school's equal opportunities policy, the practical implications of this will vary from one locality to another and will depend upon community links, communication and trust. In some communities, mixed sex work may be seen as quite acceptable provided that certain rules about clothing are upheld. In others, single sex provision will be needed if all are to have real access to the curriculum.

Who teaches which activities? Does the staffing in the department provide all pupils with role models?

Given that ethnic minority groups are under-represented in teaching generally, this is likely to be replicated within most physical education departments. In mixed sex schools there is likely to be a gender mix within the department, but how far does deployment of staff help or hinder equal opportunity policies?

How many male staff teach dance, for example? Some Year 9 boys recently declined to take part in a dance lesson taught by the senior female teacher. They were sent to the male head of department. When he remonstrated with them one responded, 'Why should we do dance, Sir? You don't and neither does Mr Cox.'

Where departmental staffing is all white, what is done to provide ethnic minority pupils with role models? In the West Midlands, the Kokuma Dance Company, a black Afro-Caribbean company with a growing national reputation, offer workshops to schools, thereby challenging both racial and sexual stereotypes and offering positive role models to black pupils. Black athletes employed as youth development officers also make significant contributions within schools, particularly those who have no ethnic minority members of staff.

What expectations do you or other teachers have of particular pupil groups? Are these justified?

Do you assume that Afro-Caribbean pupils will excel in sport? that Asian pupils will be poor?
How well-informed are you about other cultures?
What assumptions do you make about male pupils? about female pupils?

The writer well remembers watching students on a group gymnastics teaching exercise early in their course. One student set up some demonstrations of good work. He asked the girls to 'make sure it looks pretty because everyone is watching' and then exhorted the boys to 'give it all you've got'. What messages was this giving to the pupils?

How do pupils behave towards each other? How do teachers behave in pupils' presence?

Do male pupils harass female pupils or vice versa? How do you deal with this?
How often do teachers use sexist or racist language?
What about pupils? How do you deal with this?

Special Educational Needs

The 1994 Code of Practice states that the needs of all pupils who may have special educational needs either throughout, or at any time during, their school careers, must be addressed. Following a decade or so of increasing integration of pupils with special educational needs into mainstream schools, all teachers are now teachers of pupils with such needs.

The 1994 Physical Education Order states that appropriate provision should be made for those pupils who need activities to be adapted in order to participate in physical education.

Many issues about meeting the needs of pupils with special educational needs apply to all subject areas, but some are clearly specific to physical education. The increased integration of pupils with special educational needs into mainstream schools has drawn attention to the fact that many pupils who have always been in mainstream education will have special needs at some point during their school career, and that a significant number of pupils will have ongoing special educational needs in the physical education context. Examples of the latter would be pupils who suffer from asthma or diabetes. They do not require adaptation of curriculum activities but do require understanding of their condition by the physical education teacher and a sensitivity to their particular needs. They are likely to require adaptation of departmental procedures. For example, rules about eating in lessons would need to be waived to ensure that a diabetic pupil was free to eat a snack at the beginning of or during a lesson.

There will be range of conditions which will affect the child's capacity to take part in physical education but which a teacher may meet only rarely if at all. These include spina bifida, Friedrich's Ataxia, cerebral palsy and muscular dystrophy. Students should be aware of sources of information about such conditions both in terms of personnel and of available literature. For example both the BAALPE 1990 publication and Sheila Jowsey's book *Can I Play Too?* (1992) give helpful outlines of the nature of various medical conditions and of the implications for physical education.

Issues

Is the condition permanent or temporary?
Is the condition stable, fluctuating or deteriorating?
Is the pupil on medication and what are the effects and implications for PE?
Are all activities accessible and/or suitable?
Does the pupil have a single or multiple disability and what are the implications?

Integrated	No special considerations apart from constant checking that the pupil is actively involved and learning rather than simply being present.
Integrated plus helper	Helper needs to have all relevant information about pupils and to be clear about what is expected. There is a fine balance between optimum help and stifling independence and limiting learning by over-supporting. Providing that insurance cover applies, helpers could be parent, student, sixth former or ancillary support.
Integrated but modified	Pupil works in the same class as peers, possibly with a helper but with modifications to equipment, rules of expected outcomes. For example, a pupil might use a sponge ball rather than a basketball or be allowed to carry the ball without being challenged.
Parallel	Pupil remains in the same location but is given different activities or tasks. For example a pupil in a wheelchair might practise manoeuvring while other pupils are practising particular gymnastics skills.
Separate	Alternative segregated activities can be provided for individuals or small groups instead of or in addition to class lessons. For example pupils with hearing impairments might have a seperate games lesson as an alternative to playing in a sports hall with poor acoustics and a lot of background noise.
Use of alternative venues	Local facilities may extend the range of activities available, e.g. hydrotherapy pools, some fitness facilities. A pupil might attend a special school for specific curriculum activities which might include physical activities.
Contract system	Regular attendance at an activity outside school may be negotiated as a substitute for attendance at particular lessons, e.g. at a BSAD club or a PHAB meeting.

Figure 7.1

Options

Provision for pupils with special educational needs may be made in a number of ways, as outlined by Jowsey (1992), see Figure 7.1.

It should be remembered that very gifted pupils also have special needs. For very high level performers, who are already training for long hours, participation in curriculum work is likely to be of little benefit. Such pupils need special treatment which could well involve allowing them to spend physical education time on homework to compensate for the time given to evening or early morning training. For others, participation can be an opportunity to apply advanced skills in a different situation or to develop aspects of planning and evaluation in the context of helping others.

Activities for Developing Awareness of Entitlement Issues

Activity A

Why?

To extend understanding of practical work with special educational needs pupils.

When?

At a stage when students are ready to consider wider issues. This issue comes under the group of competences described as 'Further Professional Development'.

How?

Students should –

- identify a pupil with special educational needs
- observe the problems presented by this pupil's disability or difficulty in learning in relation to physical education
- identify adaptations to methods, material or the environment which are needed to help the pupil to gain access to the normal curriculum
- find out what sources of help are available within the school for supporting teachers in meeting these needs
- identify ways in which teaching content, method, style or resources/equipment have been adapted and how successful this has been.

Follow-up discussion

How is special needs interpreted?

What provision is made for pupils identified as having a special need?

How is the department responding to the recommendations of the Code of Practice?

What possible strategies could be adopted with this pupil and what would the implications be for resourcing and teaching approaches?

Activity B

Why?

To further students' understanding of equal opportunities in the school context and to consider how issues which arise in practice might be addressed.

When?

At any time after introductory work has raised student awareness of issues.

How?

Students should consider one or more of the following case studies and consider what issues arise and how they would address them. If possible they should discuss available options with different members of school staff.

CASE STUDY A

Physical education is taught to mixed sex groups. Ravinder brings a note from her parents explaining that Ravinder is embarrassed at having to take part in physical activities in front of boys and that they would prefer her to be excused from PE in the future.

CASE STUDY B

The class has been asked to get into pairs and three pupils are left over, James, Sukh and Marianne. The teacher tells James to join up with one of the others. James says that he would rather work in a three with Mark and Tim. The teacher insists. James retorts, 'I'm not going to work with a Paki or a girl'.

CASE STUDY C

Dance is taught to mixed sex groups in Years 7 and 8. After initial difficulties in getting the pupils to work together, girls were given permission to wear tracksuit bottoms or tights. One morning, when asked to stand up and find a space, the boys remain seated in a group. When asked again their spokesperson says that they are on strike because the uniform rules discriminate against them.

CASE STUDY D

The Year 9 soccer team are due to play an away match against another school which they need to win in order to keep their current high position in the local league. On the day before the match the teacher receives two letters from parents explaining that they would prefer their sons not to play because 'those black kids from X school are likely to beat them up afterwards'.

Follow-up discussion

What are the issues involved?

What are the options open to the teacher?

What would be the implications of choosing one option rather than another?

What strategies would the students choose and why?

Activity C

Why?

To further understanding of the impact of the curriculum on pupils.

When?

At any time.

How?

Use time with a tutor group to conduct a survey of pupil likes and dislikes within the physical education curriculum. If possible, talk to boys and girls separately. Find out which activities pupils like and why, and which they dislike and why. Find out what might make unpopular activities more popular (if anything). Find out what activities pupils are involved in outside school.

Questions for discussion

Which activities are enjoyed by which pupils?

Are preferences related to gender? to ability? to cultural group?

How do you account for this?

What strategies might you use to make activities a more positive learning experience for all pupils? Teaching groupings? Content? Teaching styles?

CHAPTER 8

Helping Students to Learn from Observation

Although observation forms a part of all initial teacher education courses and is usually introduced early on in the student's time in school, it is all too often seen as unhelpful by students and consequently dismissed as a waste of time. Usually when this happens it is because the observation has not been guided sufficiently clearly for it to be worthwhile. At one level everything looks rather familiar – to be expected since students have been pupils themselves. At another it may all look smooth and straightforward as an experienced teacher makes what is really a very complex process look deceptively simple. Above all, students are often preoccupied with needing to prove to themselves that they can survive a lesson as a teacher, and see observation as an obstacle coming between them and the achievement of this.

Why observe?

Observation can enable students to:

- increase awareness of the ability range within different classes
- begin to see the classroom as a teacher rather than as a pupil
- begin to analyse what goes on in lessons
- increase awareness of different ways of teaching
- increase awareness of the use of language and of the voice
- increase awareness of equal opportunity considerations
- increase awareness of management activities
- identify things about which they are not clear and with which they need further help
- increase awareness of standards set by teachers
- learn about timing and pace
- improve subject knowledge
- increase understanding of the impact of teacher expectations or particular teacher behaviour.

Some of the observation activities have been planned to help student learning during the early stages of their preparation for teaching, but most would also be valuable as INSET activities for more experienced teachers as well as for NQTs. It is worth remembering that not all of the activities necessarily involve observation of a complete lesson. This is especially important if they are to be used by members of a department when time is at a premium. Observation of the relevant part of several lessons can produce useful data to inform discussion.

How to observe

Students need help in order to make the most of observation and to appreciate its value. Hagger, Burn and McIntyre (1993) identify a number of reasons why students may find observation of limited use.

- A fluent and polished performance by an experienced teacher may look easy with the consequence that the student observing remains unaware of the factors which have contributed to the smooth running lesson.
- Students bring their own experience as pupils to the observation instead of looking from a teacher's point of view. Having spent thousands of hours in classrooms, gymnasia and playing fields as pupils, the transition to being a teacher is not automatic.
- Students may have strong preconceptions of the sorts of teachers they want to be. Any teacher not matching these preconceived notions may be dismissed as having nothing to teach them.
- Students are understandably anxious to prove themselves as teachers and may want to get on with learning from their own practice rather than from that of others.

Most of the above can be solved by carefully and clearly targeted observation, based in the first instance on aspects of teaching which students have identified as areas which they need to learn about.

All too frequently observation is seen as necessarily sitting at the side making copious notes. There are times when note-taking throughout the lesson can be useful; however it is not the only way of undertaking observation tasks. The best way of carrying out the observation should be one consideration when setting it up. While observation is generally interpreted as student observing teacher, student and teacher both observing another student is a very profitable activity. It enables the teacher to give feedback to the observing student during the lesson and to explain or to suggest alternatives at the time. Some practical suggestions for observation activities to raise awareness of different aspects of teaching and learning are given at the end of this chapter.

Observation may also be used to help the student to develop particular teaching skills and to understand the factors which affect their use. If this is the purpose of the observation, students should be clear about the skill or expertise which they would like to acquire or strengthen in their own teaching. Arrangements should be made for them to observe a teacher in a lesson when those particular skills or expertise are most likely to be in evidence. For example, if the student needs to see effective questioning techniques in practice, then it would be sensible to choose a lesson where these are likely both to be in use and reasonably easy to observe. Indoors will be more suitable than out on the field because it will be easy to hear both questions and answers. A lesson such as a gymnastics lesson using a problem-solving teaching style will be more appropriate than a swimming lesson using largely practice or reciprocal style teaching.

The student should be encouraged to ask the teacher for relevant information about the class to help to make sense of the observation, such as work in progress, aims of the lesson, information about individual pupils. A time should be arranged for a follow-up discussion, bearing in mind that the sooner this takes place after the lesson the more useful it is likely to be.

Since it can be threatening for some teachers to have an inquisitive student in their lesson asking questions afterwards, some advice is often needed if the discussion afterwards is to be productive. Students may find the following guidelines helpful:

It is generally useful to ask questions that focus on –

- the teacher's successes or achievements;
- the actions taken by the teacher to achieve those things;
- the teacher's reasons for taking the actions he or she did.

It is useful to avoid –

- questions that are framed as generalisations. A generalised question such as 'Do you always introduce partner balances like that?' is likely to lead to bland generalisations in reply, whereas, 'I noticed that you made the whole class practise two very specific balances before you gave out the task cards. Can you tell me why you introduce the topic that way?' is likely to produce answers that are more helpful.
- closed questions in which you attempt to test your own ideas, e.g. 'Did you cut short the tackling practice because they were finding it difficult?' is not as helpful as 'Can you tell me why you cut short the tackling practice?'
- moving on to another point after a brief response rather than helping the teacher to talk about the ordinary everyday things that he or she usually takes for granted. Never be afraid of saying 'Could you tell me a little more about that?'
- asking 'Why didn't you?' as this puts teachers on the defensive and leads them to try to justify their teaching rather than to reveal their thinking.

A successful discussion is one in which –

- the teacher does most of the talking;
- the teacher explains his or her actions but does not feel the need to justify them;
- the questions are about specific things in the lesson observed;
- the focus is on what went well in the lesson;
- you learn much more than you could have done from simply observing the lesson.

Practical Activities

Activity A

Why?

To encourage students to appreciate factors which affect the amount of activity or learning time within different PE lessons.

When?

At any time in the course.

How?

Use the grid shown as Figure 8.1. You could adjust the categories to make them specific to a particular lesson or activity if you wish, for example removing the listening to music category for lessons where this would not apply. Every 30 seconds, tick the category which describes what the pupils are doing. Total the ticks at the end of the lesson to give a crude analysis of the balance of time spent in learning-related activity, management-related activity or other categories.

Category	Tallies	Total
Learning: Physically active		
Learning: Watching demonstration		
Learning: Listening to explanation		
Learning: Answering questions		
Management: Listening to instructions		
Management: Moving equipment		
Listening to music		
Other		

Figure 8.1

(a) Ask each student to do this activity with a different class and teacher and compare the results.
(b) Ask students to do this activity in each other's lessons, either each observing the other teaching the same activity or observing contrasting activities.
Note This activity can also be done using a time-line, simply marking waiting time, listening time and activity time and then calculating the percentage of the lesson spent on each.

Follow-up discussion

What differences were found?

How do you account for these?

- Class size?
- Teaching style?
- Nature of the activity?
- Learning objectives for lesson?
- Pupil behaviour?
- Teacher management skills?
- Lesson context (e.g. inside, outside, weather conditions)?

Activity B

Why?

To increase awareness of how different pupils experience the same lesson.
To increase awareness of the need for differentiation.

When?

At any time, but probably early in the course.

How?

Choose two pupils to be the focus of the observation, preferably of different abilities. Use the grid shown as Figure 8.2. Every 30 seconds tick the category which describes what each is doing. Compare the tallies for the two pupils at the end of the lesson.

Category	Tallies	Total
Active on-task successfully		
Active on-task unsuccessfully		
Off-task but working constructively		
Off-task but not disrupting anyone else		
Off-task and distracting other pupils		

Figure 8.2

Each student should complete the activity for a different lesson. If possible try to arrange this so that one student observes a lesson where all pupils, whatever their ability, will find it relatively easy to remain on-task while another observes in a situation where this is more challenging for the teacher.

Follow-up discussion

What differences were observed?

How do you account for these?

- pupil physical ability
- pupil comprehension
- pupil attitude
- nature of tasks
- difficulty of tasks.

What strategies could be used to increase the amount of time spent on-task by all pupils?

Activity C

Why?

To focus attention on aspects of pupil management.
To increase awareness of use of language and voice.
To begin to see the learning environment as a teacher rather than as a pupil.
To increase awareness of different ways of teaching.

When?

At any time, but probably early in the course.

How?

Answer some or all of the following questions:

1. *How does the teacher get the pupils' attention?* Note the different ways used, when they are used and how effective they are.

  – 'Stop'
  – Blows whistle
  – Raises voice
  – Waits for silence
  – Calls a name
  – Other ways

2. *How does the teacher reward pupils?* – praising the individual, praising the individual in front of the class, asking the individual to demonstrate, awarding of merit mark (or school equivalent).

3. *How does the teacher discipline pupils?* The student should make notes of the

- – nature of the incident and the activity in which it occurred
- – teacher's response
- – reaction of the individual or group concerned
- – reaction of the rest of the class

4. *How are pupils organised into teams/groups?*

- – Teacher chosen?
- – Pupils chosen? Collectively or by named individuals?
- – By ability? In friendship groups?

Follow-up discussion

What was observed?

How effective was it?

Why was it effective? Would it work with all classes? In all contexts?

Why was it not effective? What would have been an alternative?

Activity C

Why?

To raise awareness of who gets the attention in the lesson.
To increase awareness of equal opportunity issues.

When?

At any time.

How?

Make a note of each occasion when the teacher speaks to an individual. Is it –

- to a girl
- to a boy
- to an able pupil
- to a less able pupil
- praise

- constructive criticism
- censure
- instruction
- question.

(a) Ask each student to do this activity with a different class and teacher and compare the results.
(b) Ask students to do this activity in each other's lessons.

Follow-up discussion

Who got most attention or was it distributed evenly?

What kinds of interaction predominated?

Was praise earned or given indiscriminately?

Were boys praised more than girls/criticised more than girls?

What lessons can be learned from this?

Activity D

Why?

To increase awareness of uses, abuses and effects of rewards and sanctions.

How?

Students should note during a specified period of time (a week?) all the different rewards and sanctions which they see in use both in PE and elsewhere, in preparation for a discussion.

Follow-up discussion

What sanctions were used?

How effective were they?

Do any conflict with other aspects of our work?, e.g. does making pupils do press ups or run round the field run counter to instilling the notion of exercise as a pleasant activity?

Could sanctions seen in other lessons be used or adapted for use in PE?

What was punished? Poor performance? Lack of effort? Poor behaviour? Were different sanctions used for different categories of misdemeanour?

What rewards were given?

What is rewarded? Performance? Effort? Behaviour? Do some pupils have more chance of rewards than others? What are the implications of this for motivation?

Activity E

Why?

To compare pupil response to different teaching approaches.

How?

Observe the same group of pupils being taught by two different teachers. A further dimension can be added if one male and one female teacher are chosen.

or

Observe the same activity being taught by two different teachers.

or

Observe the same group of pupils being taught two contrasting activities, e.g. rugby and dance.

Make a note of a selection from, depending on the chosen activity:

- who react most positively in each part of each lesson and who, if any, react negatively;
- who receives most teacher attention;
- the sort of attention given – praise, censure, feedback, criticism;
- how much feedback is given to individuals, to groups, to the whole class.

Follow-up discussion

What differences were observed?

How can they be accounted for?

CHAPTER 9

Collaborative Teaching

Collaborative teaching refers to students sharing the teaching of a lesson with the teacher, or to students working as a pair to teach a lesson. Often students and mentors work together in a lesson. Formalising the organisation of the lesson allows negotiation of the roles of these people within the working space. It is useful to clarify the different roles, especially for the student who needs to be aware of such things as authority shifts. It is especially important that the student teacher has a clearly defined responsibility within the lesson. In some schools consideration needs to be given to how best to introduce pupils to what will be a new way of working. In others, extra adults in a classroom are part of everyday school life and team teaching will need no special explanation.

The nature and form of collaborative teaching will change during the course of a student placement. Early on it can be used to provide a supportive and protected environment within which the student can begin to develop teaching skills. This may mean that the mentor takes the major responsibility for the class while the student plays a minor role either by looking after a small group of pupils or by leading a small section of the lesson. Later the student can be expected to play a more significant role both at the planning and the implementation level. Collaborative work is now used to extend teaching skills, to enable the student to try out 'high risk' strategies or to maximise benefits for pupils.

Possible roles

1. *One teaches the whole lesson while the second acts as support teacher for a specific group of pupils (special needs, disruptive, gifted).*
For some collaborative teaching activities, joint planning is essential. For others, such as the example given here, while desirable, it is not essential. The student will however need the teacher's lesson plan well in advance so that the student can plan his or her contribution. The teacher will plan the lesson for the whole class, asking the student to work with a specific

group of pupils – possibly high achievers, possibly pupils who find the work difficult. Using the teacher's plan as a guide, the student plans for one of these groups, using extension activities, modified tasks or for different outcomes appropriate for the group being taken. The teacher leads the lesson with the student working with the agreed group of pupils.

Jane's Year 8 gymnastics group has four pupils who attend the local gymnastics club several times a week and are considerably more experienced than the rest of the class. She agrees with the teacher that the class will work on flight and she will take the four pupils throughout the lesson, extending the tasks set by the teacher so that these pupils are challenged, for example:
(a) the class is asked to get onto or off a bench using flight onto or from hands. Jane asks her group to use a two-foot take off and to get the body completely inverted, resulting in overswing activities; she then asks them to choose their take off but to follow their chosen activity with another flight action, resulting in arab spring using the bench to push off followed by a turning jump and handspring followed by dive forward roll.
(b) the class is asked to choose three actions involving flight and link them, including actions of their own choosing if they wish. Jane's group link an arab spring with a flic flac (with support from Jane) followed by, in some cases, a straight jump and a dive roll and in others a full turn jump into a dive roll.

Jane's comment afterwards:
'I think that what this brought home to me was that there were these girls with advanced skills and that they could actually use the skill in the lesson. OK so if I were on my own I wouldn't have been able to be there supporting the flic flacs but they could have done all the other things. I don't think I would have necessarily thought of suggesting some of them before. I'd just have seen these kids performing with their legs straight and their toes pointed and quite enjoying it because it's easy and they're good at it, but I wouldn't have thought about whether they were being stretched.'

2. *The teaching of the lesson is shared equally between the two, having agreed beforehand who is going to introduce and develop each part. The student selects the sections of the lesson with which he or she feels most comfortable.*

Teacher and student plan the lesson together, with the teacher explaining the different factors which are taken into account at each stage and the various strategies and alternatives which will be used at each stage. The teacher's planning is thus made explicit to the student. After planning, decide how the teaching is going to be shared. Because this activity will be early on in the student teacher's training he or she should be invited to choose the section of the lesson he or she would like to lead.

> I had watched X teach several groups but it was only when we sat down and talked through how the lesson had been planned that I realised just how much I had taken for granted. I hadn't appreciated that for each task there were about six possible follow-ups and he just chose the most suitable one when he saw how they were getting on. Then there were another load of possibilities for the next thing and so on. I hadn't realised how carefully each group had been put together so that not only were they fairly similar ability but certain pupils had been kept apart, not only in different groups but working in a different part of the space. He had just automatically thought through all the possible problems. It made me realise now much planning I needed to do.

3. *One takes responsibility for distributing/managing resources while the second is responsible for explaining tasks.*

> Two students organise a 'circus' of activities for a large group of pupils where there is only one space available. One explains the tasks, starts and stops the activities and gives appropriate feedback after each. The other sets out equipment at each station before the lesson, checks that it is put down/away properly after each activity and that enough is ready for the next group. He or she also takes responsibility for putting everything away at the end.

4. *A lesson with differentiated tasks is planned. One takes responsibility for explaining the tasks. The two students or the student and the teacher share the support for the different tasks.*

Student and teacher plan a lesson which involves different groups being engaged on different tasks, making considerable demands on observation and management skills. They teach the lesson together with the student setting the tasks, having agreed that the student will 'look after' a specified number of groups once activities are under way. In subsequent lessons, the student's responsibility for groups increases while the teacher's lessens.

> Judith has a mixed ability Year 9 group for gymnastics. Some pupils are quite able and will want to continue with gymnastics as a GCSE practical option. Others lack confidence although they can be motivated provided that tasks and apparatus are suitable. Judith feels that setting the same task and expecting a differentiated outcome has been successful up to a point but that it is now only challenging the more able at the expense of putting off some of the others. She does not feel that she can keep an eye on everyone if they are all being asked to do different things. She plans a lesson in which there will be a choice of six tasks, making different physical demands and involving different kinds of apparatus. For the first lesson she looks after two groups, including one who are learning vaulting skills which need her support and another working within her line of sight. The teacher looks after the other four

groups. For the second lesson the group responsibility is shared equally between teacher and student and then the student gradually assumes responsibility for the whole class with the teacher acting as support.

5. *Working with a pair of students, one student teaches while both mentor and second student observe with a pre-identified focus.*
This can lead to a productive three way discussion after the lesson. It can be a threatening activity for the student who is teaching and they should not be pressurised into taking part. It will be less threatening if they are able to choose the focus, or if they give the observers a choice of possibilities.

Jason asks his partner Matthew and his mentor Janet to observe his interactions with different pupils during a lesson. He has been trying to give all pupils their fair share of his attention but wants to know whether both sexes are being treated evenly and whether he spends too much time with particular ability groups.

He comments afterwards:
'The observation and discussion were really useful. Even though I knew what they were looking at and so was especially conscious of who I was talking to when, I still ended up spending about four minutes with one group of boys who had been noisy but whose performance was really pretty good. Meanwhile I had been completely unaware of just how switched off three of the girls at the end were – they were just as capable as the boys but had got fed up with just getting on with it and being ignored by me.'

6. *Working with the teacher to improve the student's subject knowledge or to enable him or her to be involved with a group to which the student might not otherwise have access, e.g. Year 11, Year 13.*
Student and teacher plan the lesson together. The teacher explains the purpose of each part of the lesson and how she plans to introduce it. Teacher and student negotiate who will lead which parts of the lesson and what the other one will do when in the supporting role, e.g. observe, help a small group.

Julian has been asked to teach a Year 7 dance group who are working on a dance based on 'The Circus'. The class is to be divided into groups, each developing a motif based upon different circus activities. Julian agrees to teach one group a short motif based upon juggling and then to develop this further, having talked it through in detail with the teacher. The teacher works with the other groups. By watching the motifs developed by them and also by watching the finished routines with a commentary by the teacher, he acquires the knowledge and confidence to tackle the same topic with a whole class in the second half of the term.

A sixth form group is working for the Leisure and Tourism BTEC. Anne's course has included a lot of sports science but little in this area. The lesson is to begin with some definitions of terms, followed by discussion of questions related to some of them. Anne introduces the terms and what they mean and the teacher then leads the discussion.

7. *Working with the teacher to give pupils opportunities which might not be possible with only one teacher present. Discuss first with the student how the lesson could benefit from the presence of two people in the room (or three if there are two students).*

One student had been helping to teach a GCSE dance group. The pupils were interested in moves involving lifts and throws but it had been difficult to give everyone experience because of the need for a teacher to be there to support and ensure safety. The teacher and the two students agreed that they would each work with a third of the class so that there could be sustained practice and so that the whole group could reach a point of competence where they could use the moves learned in the future when they only had one teacher in the room. The learning possibilities were thus extended beyond what would have been feasible normally.

David has a group of 22 Year 8 pupils for swimming including four non-swimmers. He has both an ASA teaching award and a life saving qualification. The class teacher works in the water taking responsibility for the non-swimmers while David teaches the rest in three ability groups. Three of the four non-swimmers are able to swim by the end of a half term block.

By planning for these roles, the experienced teacher no longer has to be seen as the authority figure and critic, but as an expert helper who can take on whatever activity suits the student's need.

8. *Teacher and student organise a lesson early in the student's course to enable him or her to practise a specific teaching skill.*
Identify with the student a skill which he or she feels needs practice, for example organising demonstrations, asking questions, organising groups. Identify the points in the lesson when the chosen skill will be needed. The student then plans these episodes and concentrates on these aspects of the lesson while the teacher teaches the rest.

Martin chose to look at the organisation of demonstrations. During a basketball lesson, he agreed with the teacher that he would plan:
(a) to demonstrate the chest pass, as revision, with a pupil;
(b) to look for a group of pupils performing this well to show to the rest of the class as reinforcement;
(c) to set up a 3 v 2 practice using a variety of passes and to explain this to the class.
It was agreed that he would need to consider:

- who demonstrated (boys, girls, more able, less able, balance over the lesson as whole)
- how to make sure that the pupils involved know what they are supposed to be showing
- where to site demonstrations for visibility and safety and where pupils would need to be positioned if they were to be able to see
- what points he would emphasise to the rest of the class
- what questions he would ask the class
- how the purpose of the demonstration would affect the balance between for example questions and explanation.

CHAPTER 10

Observing Lessons and Giving Feedback

Observation of students teaching followed by an oral or written debrief has long been a feature of the initial teacher education process. The extent to which teachers have been involved in this in the past has varied. Some institutions have visited students weekly and taken most of the responsibility for observation and feedback. Others have encouraged teachers to supplement the feedback provided by the higher education tutor by their own observations. Some schools have developed systems to ensure that all students are observed by staff in the relevant department. In implementing the requirements of Circular 9/92 the responsibility for observation and feedback has passed largely to teachers in school. This chapter will look at the purposes and outcomes of observing and debriefing students, at the processes involved and at different approaches to structuring written feedback.

Why observe?

Observation of student teaching is undertaken for two main purposes although making a clear distinction between them is rather artificial. The first is for assessment purposes. This may provide diagnostic assessment of students' teaching to help them to analyse their teaching, to recognise strengths, to identify areas of weakness and develop strategies for improvement and to set targets for further development. It may provide a summative assessment of the student's current level of competence either at an intermediate point in a placement or at the end.

The second reason for observing student teaching is to help them to improve without the pressure of feeling that they are being assessed. While judgements will still inevitably be made, these observations are not assessments but are a part of the task of mentor as 'critical friend'. The focus of the assessment may well be chosen by the student. Evidence from students themselves and from inspections of the early days of partnership courses suggests that teachers give students good support and help with classroom management and with the development of basic teaching skills, but are less good at promoting the further development of student competence by continuing to analyse and set targets after the student has demonstrated a basic competence level. Where this happens, the potentially good student will 'plateau' at an early stage in their placement and will not make the progress of which they are capable.

For some teachers, the experience of providing written feedback may be new although they will have debriefed students orally in the past. While oral feedback has some value because of its immediacy, students value written feedback because oral comments are too often forgotten!

> I personally liked a written report with good points and points to work on.

Much as they like positive feedback, students also want constructive criticism.

> Remarks were positive but not useful because there were aspects of my teaching that a more experienced head would have put right immediately.

> They (the teachers) have not really been at all critical when I know there are several things I really need to work hard on. It would have been easy for me to cruise through and pass my TP without feeling urged to improve every aspect of teaching.

Thinking about the possible outcomes of effective debriefing should be in the context of OFSTED feedback on inspections of secondary partnership courses which suggests that mentors are particularly effective in helping students with class management and are able to help to develop basic teaching skills. Where there are weaknesses, these lie in the mentor's ability to encourage the students to continue to develop and fulfil their potential rather than remain at a level of basic competence.

Some outcomes

- development of basic teaching competence
- development of awareness of pupils
- ideas for extending personal repertoire of teaching skills and styles
- improvement or further development of existing skills
- increased awareness of further professional development issues
- appreciation of potential for application of strategies with other classes or in other schools
- appreciation of alternatives
- appreciation of limitations of strategies used
- interim or final assessment of student's current strengths and weaknesses.

The process

Supporting student learning through lesson observation and feedback is a cyclical process as illustrated in Figure 10.1.

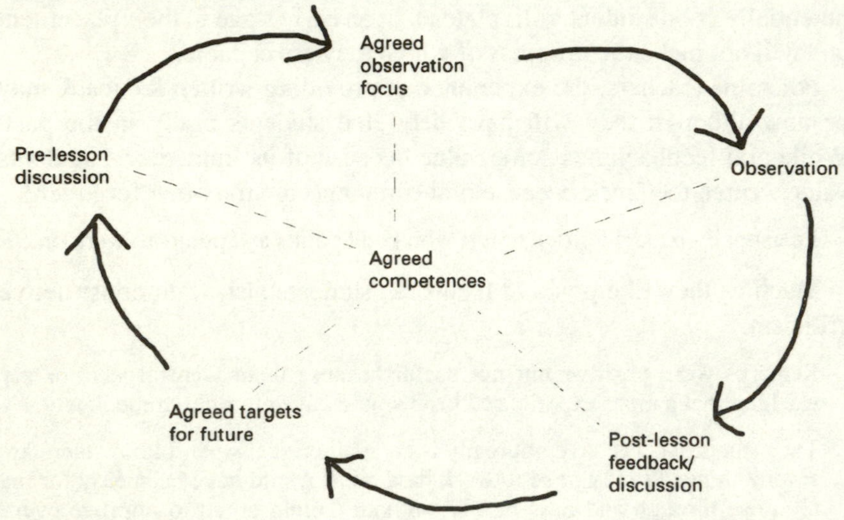

Figure 10.1

Pre-lesson discussion

The nature and length of this will depend upon several factors such as time available, student needs and the relationship between student and observer. At an early stage in a student's placement it may be important to spend some time looking at what has been planned, especially if it is in an area identified as one where the student lacks knowledge or confidence. If this is not done, the student may well be more concerned with what the observer thinks about the lesson content than with his or her own teaching. It will also be important to agree a focus for the observation. For example students in their early days in school are invariably concerned about managing and controlling pupils and will need reassurance or practical help in this area. It would therefore be counterproductive to choose a different focus which failed to address the student's concerns.

In a small school where there is constant contact between mentor and student or where there is a climate in which people are often in other teacher's lessons, 'popping in' to observe a lesson becomes part of routine and needs little formal setting up. The nature of many PE departments, where staff are together in the PE staffroom for much of the time, is such that there is often regular informal contact. Where students are placed in a large school, maybe on more than one site, student and mentor may meet less frequently, especially if the mentor has other responsibilities which takes him or her out of the department. In such a situation, some pre-lesson discussion becomes more important so that the student can outline the aims for the lesson and how he or she intends to achieve them.

It is equally important to discuss how the lesson observation is to be carried out. This is particularly true of the early days of a student placement. The assumption from the student is likely to be that the observer will sit quietly at the side, write notes, and not interfere! Any deviation from this may well cause considerable concern and an assumption that something has gone wrong. It may however be appropriate to work with the pupils at some point to gain a clearer insight into their understanding or to simply listen to their discussion. The behaviour of the observer will also vary depending upon the purpose of the observation. If the mentor is undertaking a formal assessment observation, then it would be inappropriate to 'interfere' in the lesson unless there were very good reason for so doing such as a potentially dangerous situation of which the student is unaware. Where the mentor is observing as a 'critical friend' in a less formal way, then there is no reason why the observation could not be combined with some involvement with the pupils.

Generally observation of the whole lesson would be assumed, since it is impossible to gain a full picture of the student's progress otherwise. There may however be occasions when a particular focus makes it appropriate to 'pop in' for one section. For example, students often find teaching in a full game much more difficult than working with practices. The student and mentor might discuss strategies to improve this, such as ways of conditioning a game, how to intervene to achieve, e.g. better distribution of the ball in football or hockey, or how to help individual players. The mentor could then agree to go and watch the last 15 minutes of the lesson to see how successful the student had been at putting some of these strategies into practice.

Agreeing the observation focus

There are many different aspects of the lesson which could be the focus for an observation and some are given below. It will be immediately apparent that to try to look at all of these in one lesson would be impossible and it would certainly be counterproductive to attempt to give feedback on more than a few. It will therefore be important to agree with the student what the observation will focus on. For a formal assessment, criteria will be laid down and will be known to both student and mentor. An overall picture will be appropriate with feedback on a number of aspects followed by target setting with respect to one or two. At other times the focus might be quite specific, particularly during the latter stages of placement where the strong student is likely to be thinking about further development of specific aspects of teaching. It will always be important to find out whether there are particular aspects of the lesson which the student is concerned about so that these can be addressed, even if all that is needed is reassurance afterwards. As mentioned earlier students are usually concerned about management and control issues early on and these will need to be addressed. Students may also have more specific concerns in this area, such as managing getting out large apparatus in the gymnasium. They may have concerns about particular pupils or groups of pupils, for example whether an able group is being pushed hard enough or how to deal with difficult behaviour from one or two individuals. They may wonder whether they are giving attention equitably during the lesson or whether some groups are receiving a disproportionate amount of time.

Discussion about observation focus clearly has to take place in the context of the expectations of specific training partnerships. For example, a scheme may have a weekly progress review based upon an observed lesson as part of the partnership agreement and there may be a standard proforma to be completed each week. Others may require a set number of observations over a number of weeks with two or three formal review points.

Observation – some questions to ask

The proformas at the end of this chapter give some indications of what the mentor might focus on. This section offers a number of questions which the mentor might ask of the lesson while observing. A useful staff development activity for a department or for a meeting of mentors from different schools (e.g. in a consortium meeting) would be to take some of these questions and identify performance or assessment indicators which might be used in making decisions about whether a student's performance is good, satisfactory or needing further work in this area. Many of these questions are also used by OFSTED inspectors in school inspections and are therefore relevant to the staff's own practice. A useful departmental staff development activity is to take some of these questions and consider what sort of evidence you would look for if asked to make a judgement about them with respect to students or to observing one's peers.

- Is the teaching purposeful?
- Is planning effective; are objectives and direction clear; is time used efficiently; is sufficient ground covered?

- Does the teaching create and sustain motivation?
- Is the content introduced with knowledge, skill and imagination; how does the student teacher seek to engage and maintain pupils' interest; what range of teaching strategies are employed to ensure that pupils apply themselves with purpose and self-confidence?
- Does the teaching cater for the abilities and needs of all pupils in the class? Are the student teacher's expectations appropriate for all pupils?
- Does the student teacher judge pupils' levels of understanding correctly; is the level of challenge in tasks appropriate and is time allowance realistic; are pupils who do not succeed at their first attempt helped and are the most able challenged?
- Are lessons managed in ways that ensure an efficient and orderly approach to teaching and learning?
- Do planned teaching styles promote the purposes of the lesson; are resources selected appropriate and have suitable modifications been made to accommodate pupils' special needs and abilities; are support teachers/other adults deployed effectively?
- Is there effective interaction between student teacher and pupils?
- Is the student teacher aware of equal opportunity issues and is there sensitivity to the needs of particular groups?
- Is evaluation of pupils' progress used to support and encourage them and to extend and challenge them appropriately?
- Does assessment enable pupils to improve their performance; how much does the teaching encourage pupils to assess their performance and strive for improvement?
- Is the student demanding worthwhile standards relative to pupils' abilities?
- Is praise and encouragement being given?
- Is progress and improvement being recognised?
- Are both good and bad points provoking comment?
- Is feedback given to individuals, groups and to the whole class?
- Are questions used to stimulate thought? to stimulate greater effort?
- Are opportunities given for repetition and practice?
- Is the student focusing upon key aspects of what is being attempted?
- Are opportunities to use demonstration used?

Post-lesson feedback/discussion

The effectiveness of observation and feedback depends chiefly upon what has been written and on the conduct of the debriefing. There are nevertheless other factors to be taken into account.

When and where? Ideally some post-lesson discussion should take place immediately after the lesson. If this is not possible then it should take place some time the same day. This will often need some forward planning. It may be possible to arrange to observe a lesson which is followed by one where both mentor and student are free. Alternatively a lesson immediately before break or lunch may enable some discussion to follow especially if both mentor and student can arrange to be free of other commitments on that occasion. Discussions should take place away from other people. A busy staffroom or PE room is not ideal. Not only is the conversation overheard by others, which may be offputting and inhibiting for both student and mentor, but interruptions are almost inevitable. An empty office or classroom is more suitable.

Giving the student the opportunity to talk about the lesson will give the mentor a lot of information both about how the student feels about the lesson and about their understanding of what went on. A general open question is often advised as a starting point:

How did you feel that went?

or

What did you feel went well?

It should perhaps be noted that one group of students identified these open questions as one of the most disliked features of tutor visits! They preferred being told! That said, the student's reaction to a lesson is essential in helping the mentor to decide how to make best use of the debrief. For example if a lesson has in the mentor's judgement gone badly, not in an unsafe way but in terms of pupil expectations and learning, the student may be devastated and upset, convinced that he or she will never make a teacher. Alternatively the student's reaction may be that he or she thought it was fine. Thus the mentor may have a confidence building job to do or may have to try to get the student to recognise that his or her expectations are not high enough and will need adjustment.

> You have just observed a basketball lesson in which a group of pupils was persistently disruptive. They did not practise as asked, frequently knocking the ball into other groups to disturb them. They complained throughout the modified game that 'This is silly'. They are all able players for whom the lesson was not sufficiently challenging. Different content would solve the problem. Most of the class had worked well. Compare the responses of these two students:
>
> *Monica:* 'That was just awful. They just didn't listen at all and they got worse and worse. It's all my fault but I don't know how to get them involved and working properly.'
>
> *Sara:* 'Well I thought it was pretty good really. That big-headed group are just a pain – I'll probably put them in detention. They need to learn that what I say goes.'

Despite the comments of the students quoted earlier in this chapter, it is most important to temper criticism with positive comments. Student morale can be very fragile. Learning to teach is probably very different from the kind of learning to which they are accustomed, where success has often come easily and been dependent largely on factors which the student was able to control. The many variables which can conspire to wreck the best laid plans – assembly finishing late; workmen arriving to paint part of the gym; the volleyballs in the back of an absent member of staff's car; only 14 pupils present when plans have been made for 30 or more – lead to frustration and bruised and battered egos. One of the most difficult tasks for a mentor is to restore confidence if a student has lost it, so this is one area where prevention is definitely better than cure!

While encouraging the student to talk while the mentor listens is undoubtedly good practice and essential if the student is to learn to assess his or her own teaching effectively, it clearly needs to be balanced with some input from the mentor. This is particularly so where a student does not appear to be aware of things which the mentor sees as serious weaknesses. If you are going to give constructive feedback remember that it should be:

- concrete and specific ('you could use these task cards with them', rather than, 'you need to give them something simpler');
- refer to actions and behaviour rather than personality ('concentrate on varying the pitch of your voice to help you sound more enthusiastic', rather than, 'you need to brighten up your personality');
- be based on factual data ('you had been talking for 15 minutes before there was any activity', rather than, 'you took too long to get going');
- be according to criteria which are known and agreed;
- understood by the student – do not assume this!
- based on a two-way discussion;
- lead to targets for future lessons.

Agreed targets for the future

The acronym generally given as advice for target setting is that targets should be SMART, i.e.

Sensible
Manageable
Attainable
Realistic
Time constrained

Structuring the observation and feedback process

In order to ensure that students are treated consistently and equitably, proformas are normally provided which are used by all schools within a particular partnership. Not only is it important that all PE students receive equitable treatment, but it is equally important that they are treated no differently from students in other subject areas unless there is good reason for this.

Given that observation is both for the assessment of the student and for supporting their learning, and that the two require rather different kinds of information, a number of institutions have provided separate observation and reporting guidelines, one to be used formatively and one for summative assessments. Of the many different guidelines available, two main approaches feature:

- a largely quantitative albeit subjective assessment by which a numerical grade is given for different aspects of the student's teaching;
- a largely qualitative assessment which relies on prose comments. These may be factual or judgemental.

Within both, the amount of detail available to guide the mentor can vary from little, if any, to copious notes explaining different levels of competence in minute detail. The following Examples A to F illustrate various methods and degrees of detail.

It is fair to say that Examples A and B are likely, in practice, to lean towards assessment rather than support. This, in practice, was the major role of the tutor, who, with a limited number of school visits, would assess student progress by watching different classes and different activity areas.

The teacher has the advantage of full-time presence in the school and therefore much more flexibility in what and how often to observe. Possibilities open up for using alternative observation approaches which target specific issues, often chosen by the student. The observation may serve to reassure, to raise awareness or to solve specific problems. These points are illustrated in Examples C to F.

EXAMPLE A

Lesson Observation Guide University of Wessex Physical Education

Student.. Observer...

School... Class................................

Lesson Description.. Date................................

Pre-lesson planning	Selection of content	☐
	Pre-lesson organisation	☐
	Choice of resources	☐
Lesson opening	Reception of class	☐
	Register	☐
Organisation	Pupils	☐
	Equipment	☐
	Timing	☐
Teaching and learning activities	Appropriateness of tasks	☐
	Challenge for pupils	☐
	Teaching strategies used	☐
	Feedback given	☐
	Outcomes	☐
	Use of voice	☐
	Positioning	☐
Interaction with pupils	Whole class	☐
	Groups	☐
	Individuals	☐
	Use of praise	☐
	Discipline	☐
Lesson ending	Closing remarks	☐
	Dismissal of group	☐
	Equipment put away	☐

Observation summary (Good points, points to work on)

Observer.. Student..

(For each box: 1 = very good 2 = good 3 = satisfactory 4 = needs further work n/a = not applicable)

EXAMPLE B

Student.. Date.........................

Class................................ Activity...

Observer...

Focus of Observation (if appropriate)...

Comments

Criteria: Preparation, lesson content, class management and organisation, teaching strategies, relationship with pupils, pupil learning

Agreed targets

Observer...................................... Student...

EXAMPLE C

A factual account of the lesson used as a basis for discussion. Note that without interpretation the account will be of limited use

9.10 Register taken in changing room.

9.20 Pupils line up outside gymnasium. A group are spoken to about their behaviour. They answer back and the whole class is sent back to the changing room. After a few minutes they return and line up again.

9.30 Pupils enter the gym. Asked to run anywhere. A lot of noise, both talking and from their feet. Are they supposed to wear trainers for gymnastics? You stop them and ask them to 'make better use of the space'. They continue to run largely in circles, but do use more of the whole area. The noise level continues to be high. You do not make any comment about this.

9.34 Pupils sit down in twos and fetch mats when you ask them to. Two pairs go and help themselves without being told. You do not stop them. You remind them not to drag the mats. You ask them to begin to practise as soon as their mat is out. Most sit down and wait for further instructions.

EXAMPLE D

Focus: Use of teacher time

Clare has heard pupils commenting about the way another teacher 'has favourites', who get all the attention in lessons. She asks her mentor to observe her and to make notes about her interactions with pupils during the lesson.

Her mentor draws a plan of where the pupils are working, as during this gymnastics lesson they will stay in the same area of the gymnasium throughout.

During the lesson she marks each time Clare addresses a pupil, using symbols as follows:

x praise
+ criticism
? asks question
– accepts answer
* other comment (including ones which could not be heard).

Discussion after the lesson looked at the following questions:

- balance between attention to boys and attention to girls and reasons for differences;
- the ability level of the pupils who received the most attention;
- the kind of attention given to different pupils.

EXAMPLE E

Focus: Involvement of specific pupils in lessons

David is finding it difficult to observe all the pupils in his teaching groups and is worried that the average boys who do not cause trouble may be missing out. He asks his mentor to observe three boys in particular.

His mentor makes notes on the three, concentrating on:

- whether they are on-task or not;
- how successful they are with the tasks set;
- whether they seem to be enjoying the work;
- whether David gives them any feedback and how often.

Discussion after the lesson looked at the boys' involvement in the lesson and David's interactions with them.

EXAMPLE F

Focus: Use of demonstrations

Judith feels that some teachers use demonstrations with no clear purpose or as a time filler at the end of a lesson. She asks her mentor to focus on her use of demonstrations during her lesson. Her mentor makes notes on:

- who is asked to demonstrate;
- when and why Judith demonstrates herself;
- the organisation of the demonstration;
- whether the pupils know what they are looking at and why;
- Judith's comment and questions during and after the demonstration.

CHAPTER 11

Assessing Teaching Competence

All initial teacher training courses involve both formative and summative assessment in some form. The issues around these forms of assessment already outlined in Chapter 6 with reference to the assessment of pupils are equally relevant to the assessment of the student teacher. The final assessment of the student not only provides a summative judgement about their current level of competence, but also contribute, directly or indirectly, to profiles which are being used increasingly to plan for the induction needs of newly qualified teachers. It therefore needs to include not only information about relative strengths and weaknesses but also information about the student's experience to date, both within the department and in the wider aspects of school life. Most partnerships will have well defined systems for the assessment of the student's teaching competence.

Partnerships will almost certainly use some kind of profiling system to support the student's progress throughout the course and to contribute to the overall assessment process. The features of most profiling systems are:

- they make an important contribution to formative assessment;
- they engage the student in the process of review and reflection;
- they involve a regular review of progress and setting of targets for the future;
- they enable the student to plan and organise their own learning.

Many are, at present, student owned. The future introduction of end of course profiles for all student teachers will obviously change this. Some partnerships use the profile as both an aid to student development and as the major assessment tool, while others see profiles as a formative process which might inform the assessment of the student but which does not constitute the whole of it.

Comparability and consistency

The assessment of student teaching has always been a complex matter because of the differences between the contexts in which students are placed, whether this be in terms of the match between school curriculum policies and student expertise, relative difficulty of teaching in different schools, variations in practice given (e.g. between a 11–14 junior high school and a 13–18 school), levels of support available and so on. Regardless of the quality of the individual mentors involved, assuring some kind of consistency of standard between anything up to 70 or 80 individuals, working almost certainly over a widely dispersed geographical area, is a major new challenge.

The descriptors of the competences provided in Circular 9/92 (DFE, 1992) have been criticised for lacking both consistency and detail. They do not follow the NCVQ model in offering explicit descriptions of levels of proficiency. This is probably just as well since the problems involved in deciding exactly what should be expected of a newly qualified teacher and in what context would be severe indeed. No indication is given of any weighting which might be attached to one competence rather than another; indeed some appear to be subsumed by others, for example if teachers are to 'maintain interest and motivation' (para. 2.4.4) one might assume that they would need to use 'appropriate rewards and sanctions' (para. 2.4.3). The phrase 'newly qualified teachers should be able to...' is open to various interpretations. Does this mean all the time with all pupils? Does it mean occasionally with an 'easy' class? Do expectations vary between these two extremes depending upon the competence being considered? All in all, the lack of detail is to be welcomed since it does allow for considerable professional judgement and sensitivity to particular situations. The implications for quality assurance and for the equitable treatment of students placed in diverse contexts do nevertheless need to be recognised and strategies put into place for addressing these important issues. Different partnerships may choose different approaches. Ongoing input from higher education tutors may provide moderation and quality assurance in one partnership. In another it may be achieved through mentors visiting each others' schools, valuable if time consuming. In another moderation meetings and use of video material to standardise approaches may be used.

Context

The context within which the assessment takes place has already been alluded to. Inevitably students will be placed in schools which make widely differing demands upon them. For some, management of pupils will be a major issue throughout their time in the school and will remain a top priority, inevitably restricting time which, in another school, might be given to addressing other competences. Students who are placed in a school which is very different from their own school experience will need a period of adjustment which may not be an issue for others. Some students will be teaching activities with which they may be relatively unfamiliar. This may well mean that, with their focus on ensuring that the content is appropriate, experimenting with unfamiliar teaching styles at the same time will be resisted. Others may be teaching theoretical work with examination classes, in addition to practical activities. Some will be teaching 11–18, some 11–16, some 13–18, others 11–14. Even on courses where time is split evenly between two schools, the final assessment will be on student performance in their second placement.

Grading levels and evidence of competence

Most final assessments are graded on a pass/fail basis with the student profile providing more detailed information about specific strengths and weaknesses. There are still a few courses which require a more detailed assessment and where the student's practical teaching competence contributes in some way to a final degree classification. The latter face added difficulties in ensuring that student assessments are equitable particularly when comparing students working in very different types of schools.

No matter what process is adopted or what form of final reporting is used, mentors will need to consider a range of evidence in coming to judgements about student performance. What kinds of evidence could be useful?

- *The student's file* – evidence of planning, subject knowledge, sensible selection of content, thought to sequencing and organisation, evidence of reflection, of observation and assessment of pupils.
- *The student's practical performance* – evidence of ability to use varied styles and strategies, to manage the learning environment, to manage and control pupils, to organise safely, to improve pupil performance, to help their learning and so on.
- *Discussions with the student* – talking to the student may reveal considerable understanding and knowledge, even where this is not always apparent in the actual teaching.
- *Activities undertaken outside timetabled lessons* – involvement in extra-curricular activities and clubs, in parents evenings, in school trips, all provide evidence of commitment and enthusiasm for the job and may provide evidence of other competences as well.
- *Student's written work* – assessment of written assignments may be

undertaken by the school or higher education institution and may be carried out during a placement or separate from it. It may therefore provide the mentor with a variety of evidence depending upon the assignment set.

- *Activities set for the student to complete* – a student may be asked to carry out some of the activities suggested in earlier chapters prior to discussion at a weekly meeting.
- *Evidence from other staff* – staff outside the PE department may work with a student either in teaching another subject or in an attachment to a tutor group.

It is important that the system used for identifying and collecting evidence is sufficiently flexible to be responsive to the stage reached by the student and to the kinds of expectations which are reasonable at any given point in training. Final assessments need to provide a record which shows that the student has reached at least the minimum standards required in the competences designated as relevant by the DFE.

Whose responsibility?

The way in which responsibility for assessment is shared between higher education and the school in partnership courses varies. In a school-centred scheme of course it will be the responsibility of the school. Where both higher education and the school are involved, the roles of each need to be clearly identified so that the contributions of the two partners complement each other rather than overlapping or leaving important issues unaddressed.

Balance between summative and formative assessment

Summative assessment in the form of a test or examination does not play a part in initial teacher education. Rather, the summative assessment takes the form of 'summing up', that is the aggregation of all of the formative assessment which has taken place. This places a responsibility upon schools to ensure that students do have ample opportunity to demonstrate the competences which are needed to be awarded a 'pass'. For example if an assessment criterion is that the student should 'show competence in teaching a range of NC activity areas' it is clearly important that the student's timetable should include a range of activities and not be restricted to one or two. This may be an issue for selection of a school for a student placement in the first place. In some partnerships, where the final placement is during a single school term, some schools have not been able to offer a broad enough experience for students because of the way their particular PE programme is organised.

Approaches to gathering the evidence needed to award a pass mark to a student vary. In some partnerships the onus is very much upon the student to present evidence and to have that particular competence signed off either by the mentor, other teacher, higher education tutor or a combination of the three. For example, one competence descriptor might be, 'Shows awareness of equal opportunity issues'. The student might present evidence through a piece of written work or through a commentary on lesson plan and implementation which highlighted equal opportunity issues which had arisen and how he or she had dealt with these. Another might be, 'Can plan lessons which take account of ability and experience of pupils'. The student could present evidence in his or her teaching file which included clearly presented plans, including content, which was appropriate for the particular class and which included differentiated activities. Lesson plans could be included for a Year 7 and a Year 10 group in the same activity which demonstrated an appreciation of the different needs of the two groups.

Figure 11.1 is an example of part of a profiling document which demands that the student provides evidence of competence which is then signed by the mentor or tutor in the relevant box.

In some partnerships a formal record of the student's competence is produced at the end of the placement, taking into account the experience which the student has gained and the formative assessment, probably in

	Excellent	Good	Satisfactory
Competence Demonstrate knowledge and understanding of NC requirements in relation to gymnastics at KS 3 & 4			
Evidence			
Competence Demonstrate ability to plan lessons for pupils of varying ability in gymnastics			
Evidence			
Competence Create and maintain a safe learning environment for gymnastics			
Evidence			

Figure 11.1

the form of written lesson evaluations, which has taken place. This record may follow the DFE competences very closely or it may use a reporting format which builds upon those previously used, with some adaptation to ensure that all the DFE competences are accommodated within it. Where courses include a number of different subject specialisms the placement report will normally be sufficiently general to accommodate all of them. This means that some further interpretation will be needed in the physical education context. In Chapter 1, the DFE competences are outlined with reference to physical education and these would be the basis of assessment. Thus, effective class management in physical education would, like that in science, need to address a whole range of safety issues, some general, some activity specific, which would not necessarily have any application within other classroom subjects.

Figure 11.2 is an example of part of a report form which a school would complete at the end of the student placement, underlining the relevant descriptor, which could include sections from more than one column and then adding a comment if needed.

Whatever the detail of individual assessment procedures, it will important for mentors and all involved in student assessment to create opportunities to observe teaching and to share thinking about its strengths and weaknesses in order to ensure that students receive equitable treatment and are judged against comparable standards.

Good	**Satisfactory**	**Needs further work**
Classroom management Knowledge is demonstrated of a wide range of classroom management procedures and their skilful implementation ensures that most lessons run smoothly.	There is evidence of the awareness of classroom management procedures and the implementation of enough of these to ensure that most lessons run smoothly.	There is evidence of a lack of awareness of classroom management procedures and/or the implementation of enough of these to enable most lessons to run smoothly.
Comment:		
Good	**Satisfactory**	**Needs further work**
Discipline Most lessons are well ordered and the instances of inappropriate pupil behaviour are noticed. The student usually reacts appropriately, sometimes deliberately ignoring misbehaviour or using rewards and sanctions sensitively, imaginatively and with good humour. Treatment of pupils shows consistency.	Most instances of inappropriate behaviour are noticed and are handled correctly, but the student has difficulty with some pupil behaviour. Generally, rewards and sanctions are appropriately and consistently administered.	Much inappropriate behaviour seems not to be noticed, but when it is, rewards and sanctions tend not to be appropriate and to be applied inconsistently.
Comment:		

Figure 11.2

Further Reading/References

General texts on mentoring

Fish, D. (1995) *Quality Mentoring for Student Teachers.* London: David Fulton.

Furlong, J., Maynard, T., Miles, S. & Wilkin, M. (1994) *The Secondary Active Mentoring Programme. Pack One: Principles and Processes.* Cambridge: Pearson Publishing.

Hagger, H., Burn, K. & McIntyre, D. (1993) *The School Mentor Handbook.* London: Kogan Page.

Tomlinson, P. (1995) *Understanding Mentoring.* Milton Keynes: Open University Press.

Vlaeminke, M. (1995) *The Active Mentoring Programme. Pack Two: Developing Key Competences.* Cambridge: Pearson Publishing.

Wilkin, M. (ed.) (1992) *Mentoring in Schools*. London: Kogan Page.

Wilkin, M. & Furlong, J. (eds) (1996) *Subject Mentoring in the Secondary School*. London: Kogan Page.

General texts on learning to teach

Capel, S., Leask, M. & Turner, T. (1995) *Learning to Teach in the Secondary School*. London: Routledge.

DFE (1992) *Initial Teacher Training (Secondary Phase), Circular 9/92.* London: DFE.

Edwards, C. & Healy, M. (1994) *The Student Teacher's Handbook*. London: Kogan Page.

Kyriacou, C. (1991) *Essential Teaching Skills*. London: Blackwell.

Moon, B. & Shelton Mayes, A. (1994) *Teaching and Learning in the Secondary School*. Milton Keynes: Open University Press.

Stephens, P. & Crawley, T. (1994) *Becoming an Effective Teacher.* Cheltenham: Stanley Thornes.

General Physical Education texts

Armstrong, N. (ed.) (1990) *New Directions in Physical Education: Vol. 1.* Leeds: Human Kinetics Books.

Armstrong, N. (ed.) (1992) *New Directions in Physical Education:*

Vol. 2. Leeds: Human Kinetics Books.

Armstrong, N. (ed.) (1996) *New Directions in Physical Education: Vol. 3*. London: Longman.

Armstrong, N. & Sparkes, A. (eds) (1991) *Issues in Physical Education*. London: Cassell.

BAALPE (1990) *Safe Practice in Physical Education*. BAALPE.

British Journal of Physical Education (1994) **25**, 4, Special edition on initial teacher training in physical education.

DES (1991) *National Curriculum Physical Education Working Group. Interim Report*. London: DES.

DES (1992) *Physical Education in the National Curriculum*. London: DES.

DFE (1994) *Physical Education in the National Curriculum*. London: DFE.

Department of National Heritage (1995) *Sport: Raising the Game*. London: Department of National Heritage.

Evans, J. (ed.) (1986) *Physical Education, Sport and Schooling*. Lewes: Falmer Press.

Hellison, D. & Templin, T. (1991) *A Reflective Approach to Teaching Physical Education*. Illinois: Human Kinetics Books.

Mawer, M. (1995) *The Effective Teaching of Physical Education*. London: Longman.

Siedentop, D. (1983) *Developing Teaching Skills in Physical Education (*Second Edition*)*. Palo Alto: Mayfield Publishing Co.

Williams, E.A. (1993) 'The Reflective Physical Education Teacher – Implications for Initial Teacher Education', *Physical Education Review*, **16**, 2, 137–144.

Physical Education topics

Special Educational Needs

BAALPE (1989) *Physical Education for Children with Special Needs in Mainstream Schools.* BAALPE.

British Journal of Physical Education (1990) **24**, 3, Special edition on Special Educational Needs in physical education.

Brown, A. and Jones, G. (1989) *Mainstreaming children with special educational needs in physical education.* University of Newcastle upon Tyne, Department of Physical Education and Sport.

Jowsey, S. (1992) *Can I Play Too?* London: David Fulton.

Equal Opportunities

Carroll, B. (1993) 'Physical Education: Challenges and Responses to Cultural Diversity', in Pumfrey, P. & Verma, G. (eds) *The Foundation Subjects and Religious Education in Secondary Schools*. Lewes: Falmer Press.

Evans, J. (ed.) (1994) *Equality Education and Physical Education*. Lewes: Falmer Press.

Leeds City Council Department of Education (1995) *Fair Play: Gender and physical education*. Leeds City Council Department of Education.

Scraton, S. (1992) *Shaping up to Womanhood: gender and girls' physical education*. Milton Keynes: Open University Press.

Assessment

BAALPE (1992) *Assessment in Physical Education*. BAALPE.

Carroll, B. (1994) *Assessment in Physical Education: A Teacher's Guide to the Issues*. Lewes: Falmer Press.

Dickenson, B. & Almond, L. (1993) 'Assessment in Physical Education: A Practical Model for Implementing National Curriculum Assessment Requirements', *British Journal of Physical Education*, **24**, 4, 22–26.

Spackman, L. (1995) 'Assessment in Physical Education', *British Journal of Physical Education*, **26**, 3, 32–34.

Spode, I. & Whitlam, P. (no date of publication) *Physical Education: Assessment, Recording and Reporting*. Dudley Physical Education Advisory Service.

Teaching styles and strategies

BAALPE (1989) *Teaching and Learning Strategies in Physical Education*. BAALPE.

Biddle, S. & Goudas, M. (1993) 'Teaching styles, class climate and motivation in physical education', *British Journal of Physical Education*, **24**, 3, 38–39.

British Journal of Physical Education (1993) **24**, 1, Special edition on teaching styles.

Mosston, M. & Ashworth, S. (1986) *Teaching Physical Education*. Ohio: Merrill.

Other references

Bilborough, A. & Jones, P. (1973) *Developing Patterns in Physical Education*. London: London University Press.

Brooks, V. et al. (1994) 'Positive Mentoring and the Novice-Expert', in Reid, I., Constable, H. & Griffiths, R. *Teacher Education Reform:*

current research. London: Paul Chapman Publishing.

Brown, G. & Wragg, E.C. (1993) *Questioning*. London: Routledge.

Butterworth, M. (1989) 'Student reactions to videotape feedback of teaching performance', *Bulletin of Physical Education*, **25**, 3, 37–41.

DES (1992) *Education in England 1990/91: The Annual Report of the Chief Inspector of Schools*. London: DES.

Harlen, W. (1991) 'National Curriculum Assessment: increasing the benefit by reducing the burden', in 'Education and Change in the 1990s', *Journal of the Educational Research Network of Northern Ireland*, **5**, February, 3–19.

OHMCI (1995) *Physical Education. A review of inspection findings 1993/4*. London: HMSO.

Perks, P. & Prestage, S. (1992) 'Planning for Learning' in Jaworski, B. & Watson, A. *Mentoring in Mathematics Teaching*. Lewes: Falmer Press.

Schools Council (1974) *Physical Education in Secondary Schools*. London: Macmillan.

Tinning, R. (1991) 'Teacher Education Pedagogy: Dominant discourses in the process of problem-solving', *Journal of Teaching in Physical Education*, **11**, 1, 1–20.

Williams, E.A. & Woodhouse, J. (1996) *From policy to practice: urban adolescents' perceptions of physical education* (forthcoming).

Index

A level 9, 17, 52
accidents 7
adult learners 2, 4
advice 4
aims 30, 32, 70
analysis 27
assessment
  of pupils 7, 14, 31, 37, 66*ff*
  of students 6, 104, 119*ff*
  principles 71
  purposes 69
  self assessment 47, 48
athletics 9, 13, 58

challenge 3, 10, 11, 42, 57
checklist 6
child development 10
class management 2, 12, 105
collaborative teaching 5, 98*ff*
command style 44, 54
comparison 27
competences 8*ff*
confidence 1, 12, 16, 53, 57
content 3, 9
continuity 9
criterion referencing 67
cultural differences 79, 80, 82, 83

dance 9, 44, 51, 58, 63, 77, 81, 83, 101, 102
decisions 10, 12, 15, 43, 45
demonstration 11, 56, 57, 59, 63, 103
department 1, 2, 4, 6
description 27
differentiation 10, 11, 37*ff*, 48, 58, 100
discussion 3, 6

effective teaching 16
EKSD 8, 14, 72, 76
equal opportunities 7, 32, 79*ff*, 89
equipment 7, 12, 36, 37
evaluation 21, 27, 47, 48, 51, 54
expectations 6, 10, 11, 83
explanations 57
extra curricular 81

facilities 7
feedback 3, 4, 5, 12, 14, 45, 46, 58, 109
formative assessment 58,67,122
further professional development 15

games 9, 20, 34*ff*, 39, 40, 42, 47*ff*, 68, 71, 76, 78, 80, 81
GCSE 9, 52, 78
gender 10
gifted pupils 15, 79, 86
GNVQ 9, 17, 52
groups 12, 35
guidance 1, 3
guided discovery 50, 54
gymnastics 9, 45, 51, 58, 63, 69, 71, 81, 99, 100

head of department 2
health 32
HEI 6

inclusion style 48, 54
independence 5, 47, 52
individual differences *see* differentation
individualised learning 52
information 6, 57
interest 13
ipsative assessment 66
IT 7, 12, 32, 72

Key Stage 8, 14, 20
knowledge 8–9

language 11, 32, 56, 89

learning environment 12, 13
learning experience 31, 33, 43
learning outcome 30, 33, 53, 54, 55, 76
lesson plans 9, 34, 37
listening 4, 56

management 12, 35, 89
material 1, 31
mentoring 2
mixed ability 57, *see* differentiation
mixed sex teaching 20, 36, 79, 81, 82, 87
monitoring 3, 6, 27

National Curriculum 8, 9
NCAT 8, 9, 14, 21, 29
non-participant 7
norm referencing 66
NQT 8, 17, 43

objectives 30
observation
- by student 3, 5, 53, 58, 89*ff*
- of student 5, 27, 104*ff*
- observation focus 107
- observation guides 113

observation task 56, 76
OFSTED 29, 81, 105, 108
organisation 35, 102
outdoor activities 8, 9

pace 39, 40, 45, 89
partnerships 1, 3, 4, 5
performance 21, 24, 26, 47, 48, 54, 66, 67
personal and social education/ development 32, 47, 54
personal qualities 16
planning by pupils 21, 25, 51, 54
planning by student 3, 9, 24, 28*ff*
PoS 8, 9, 32, 76
practice 45, 46, 47, 48
practice style 11, 45, 54
pre-lesson discussion 30, 106
preparation *see* planning
problem solving 11, 32, 51, 54
process model 20, 21, 24
profiling 119, 123
progress 5, 6
progression 28, 41*ff*, 48, 66, 67, 70
pupil learning *see* learning
pupil grouping 24, 41, 35

questions to students 30, 31, 35
questioning of pupils 50, 56, 59, 102
questioning by students 91

reciprocal teaching 11, 19, 46, 54
record keeping 14, 72, 73, 74, 75
records of achievement 14, 68, 72
reflective practice 17–20
relationships 15
reporting 14, 15, 76, 78
resources 12, 41
review 5
rewards 13
role models 2, 83

safety 12, 13, 27, 44, 50, 58
sanctions 7, 13
schemes of work 9, 14, 32, 37
selection 6
self check style 47, 54
single sex teaching 20, 36, 79, 80, 82
skills 12, 45
social skills 46
special educational needs 15, 79, 80, 84*ff*
student activity ideas 53*ff*, 76*ff*, 86*ff*, 92*ff*
student learning 1, 5, 28
subject application 9*ff*
subject knowledge 8–9, 53, 89, 100
summative assessment 68, 122
support 1, 3
swimming 9, 47, 63, 68, 71, 102
syllabus *see* schemes of work

target setting 6, 105, 111
tasks 31, 57, 58
task setting 56
teaching activities 31
teaching points 31, 47, 61
teaching strategies 11, 56*ff*, 91
teaching styles 10, 11, 35, 40, 43*ff*, 91
team teaching *see* collaborative teaching
timing 45, 89

units of work *see* schemes of work